TENSION

MASTERING THE SUPERPOWER OF PARADOX-AWARE LEADERSHIP

JARED OATES

Publishing support provided by
Ignite Press
55 Shaw Ave. Suite 204
Clovis, CA 93612
www.IgnitePress.us

ISBN: 979-8-9933447-0-6
ISBN: 979-8-9933447-1-3 (E-book)

For bulk purchases and for booking, contact:

Jared Oates
https://thelpc.com

Library of Congress Control Number: 2025920525

Cover design by Orlando Salazar
Edited by Cathy Cruise
Interior design by Jetlaunch

FIRST EDITION

TENSION

For Deniece—the person at the heart of all my whys.

Acknowledgments

All of us stand on the shoulders of giants. I gratefully acknowledge the work of many researchers and writers whose work has influenced my understanding. These are just a few, in no particular order: Brené Brown, Stephen M. R. Covey, Roger Martin, Daron Acemoglu, James A. Robinson, Simon Sinek, Brian Emerson, Kelly Lewis, Wendy K. Smith, Marianne W. Lewis, John Doerr, Ben Hardy, Dan Sullivan, and Jim Collins.

I am grateful to key friends who generously gave their time to review my manuscript. They saw things I could not and their feedback made the work better: Cathy Fyock, Luke Jensen, Johnny Luo, David Hatch, and Brett Gilliland.

Table of Contents

Introduction xi

Part 1: The Basic Idea

Chapter 1: The Cost of Choosing Sides 3
Chapter 2: Embracing Productive Tension 12

Part 2: Everyday Paradoxes in Leadership (Practical Examples)

Chapter 3: Strength and Vulnerability in Leadership 25
Chapter 4: Caution Versus Confidence 31
Chapter 5: Personal Goals Versus Team Goals in Leadership 37
Chapter 6: Measurable Versus Qualitative Goals 44
Chapter 7: Flexibility Versus Grit 53
Chapter 8: Cocreation Versus Directional Clarity 60
Chapter 9: Incremental Versus Impossible Goals 67
Chapter 10: Empathy Versus Accountability 73

Part 3: The Practice of Paradox-Aware Leadership

Chapter 11: Naming Your Paradoxes 81

Chapter 12: Applying Paradox-Awareness with
The Leadership Progress Cycle 91

Part 4: Clarifying Your Goals

Chapter 13: Defining Your Personal Purpose 103

Chapter 14: Setting Goals with Alignment 112

Part 5: Conclusion

Chapter 15: Paradox Is Personal 127

About the Author 143

Introduction

It became vivid and personal the day my mother-in-law declared we would no longer talk about politics. Ever. You've likely felt it too—around the holiday dinner table, in workplace meetings, inside group chats, or even just scrolling through the news. The world feels polarized—pulled apart. Voices grow louder, positions harden, and conversations that once felt safe now seem like minefields. It's not just happening out there in the headlines. It's in your family. Your friend circle. Your neighborhood. Your workplace.

You may be aware of how a polarized debate over the British exit from the European Union (Brexit) tore at the social fabric of the UK—leaving scars so deep that even mentioning the word would ruin a perfectly good tea. You may be aware of how India's political landscape fractured along religious lines. No matter where in the world you live, the reach of the US economy is such that you will have seen and been affected by the intensifying cycles of division between conservative and progressive leaders that have convulsed the United States. Key leaders on each side have sought not merely to prevail, but to utterly defeat and discredit one another. The costs, in terms of stalled progress, damaged relationships, and lost trust, are staggering.

As technological change accelerates, you've likely seen clashes between colleagues advocating for either innovation or stability. Innovation advocates dismiss traditionalists as unimaginative or obsolete—accusing them of parking the team bus safely in the mud. Stability advocates fire back that constant disruption threatens to steer the bus straight off a cliff. Both sides defend their perspectives as essential truths. Each side waits impatiently for the pendulum of power to swing their way so they can lock in their gains and lock out the other side. Neither side considers their legacy of confusion and resentment.

You can see it in environmental conflicts, where passionate conservationist leaders lock horns with determined advocates of economic growth. In places like Brazil, Indonesia, and Canada, debates over natural resource use frequently devolve into zero-sum contests, leading to bitter divides, policy paralysis, and social unrest.

The most troubling examples are local and personal. They keep people you know from actually seeing one another. You've probably watched up close how polarized thinking fractures relationships and freezes progress. You may have worked with managers who became so fixated on building positive relationships that they couldn't seem to hold people accountable—or others who left scorched earth behind every time they gave feedback. You may have seen micromanagers who seemed obsessed with control, or permissive leaders who avoided hard conversations until things fell apart. You may have worked with colleagues who thrived on change and disruption, pushing boundaries in ways that felt destabilizing, or watched bold plans stall out in the hands of a teammate whose instinct for risk-avoidance slowed progress.

All the situations I've described here might look unique on the surface, but they share a common root: **polarized leadership**. Opposing instincts taken to extremes, hardened into habits. Polarized leaders get fixated on one good thing and ignore something else that's also important.

Here's the good news: You can master a leadership mindset shift that will harness the energy of all these conflicts for good.

What if, instead of choosing sides, you learned to live and lead *within* the tension? What if you could see the deeper truth inside each polarized position—and help others do the same?

That's the promise of paradox-aware leadership.

A paradox is a situation where two good things seem to pull in opposite directions. A paradox-aware leader is someone who can see both good things and knows how to draw energy from the tension between them.

The "tension" this book is about is like the tuned tightness on the string of a guitar or a violin. I'm not using the word like you might to describe the feeling of a relationship that's turned abrasive or sour. I'm not talking about persistent interpersonal bickering, or office politics. I'm also not using it in the way you might describe unspoken sexual interest driving action in a romantic comedy. I'm using the word "tension" to describe a creative stress that works the same way weights provide resistance to build muscle. It's a bit uncomfortable, but absolutely necessary to progress.

This book will give you a practical way to make sense of the conflict and the complexity around you—not by resolving it prematurely, but by learning to see the deeper pattern within it. Paradox-aware leadership invites you to ask a powerful question when conversations feel stuck: *What is this person fighting FOR?* Not just what they're pushing against. Not just what frustrates you about them. But what value or vision lies underneath their intensity.

That question changes everything.

Suddenly, the leader who looked like a micromanager becomes someone fighting for excellence. The colleague who seemed like a chaos agent just wants possibility. The colleague who felt hyper-cautious deeply wants stability. The accountability-averse manager wants belonging. When you see that, you can speak to it. You can meet people in that shared space and lead them somewhere new.

Paradox-aware leadership doesn't mean never taking a stand. It means standing with clarity, compassion, and the courage to hold multiple truths at once. It's not the easy path—but it is the only one that leads to deep trust, real innovation, and solutions that last.

Paradox-aware leadership is a superpower because it is currently so very rare and because its impact is so dramatic. The powerful impulse to quickly resolve or avoid the discomfort of paradox is strong enough that only the exceptional or well-trained leader leans into it—let alone learns to harness its power. Paradox-aware solutions are, by definition, nonobvious. You have to believe they are there to put in the work to find them. Only the skilled leader looks and persists long enough.

This book is written for leaders, coaches, and trainers who are willing to hope and strive, even though they face barriers that seem insurmountable. It's for people who feel frustrated and blocked, but still have lofty goals and a conviction that there must be a way to achieve them.

It's not written for any particular ideological or political group. But if your politics or ideology have a hard-line or fundamentalist flavor, this book is probably not for you. No hard feelings—you just won't enjoy it.

It's not written for leaders from any specific religion or faith tradition, but there is a spiritual dimension to paradox-awareness. If spirituality is abrasive to you, this book is likely not your jam.

The ideas are transnational and cross-industry. If you detect a US or a tech-centric lens, please forgive the limits of my perspective. I feel most authentic sharing the stories I know best.

Here's what to expect:

In **Part 1: The Basic Idea (Chapters 1-2),** you will learn to recognize and respect paradoxes, and to navigate complexity with clarity, creativity, and compassion. You'll learn to hold ambiguity without anxiety, conflict without contempt. You'll see why your leadership has this transformative potential—to thrive in productive tension. You can become precisely what's needed in our deeply divided world.

Part 2: Everyday Paradoxes In Leadership (Chapters 3-10), presents seven key paradoxes that are already at work in your life and leadership. Chapter by chapter, tension by tension, you'll have a chance to see what it looks like to use paradox as your own superpower. You'll see how these ancient ideas aren't just philosophical curiosities. They're urgent, current, and useful. These seven paradoxes are a sample, not a definitive set. As far as I know, there is no limit to the number of possible paradoxes.

Part 3: The Practice of Paradox-Aware Leadership (Chapters 11-12), gives you a way to apply your new knowledge of paradox with two simple models: the first one for recognizing and naming the paradoxes in your own life and work, and the second one for finding those breakthrough paradox-aware solutions. This second model is a simple and repeatable process called The Leadership Progress Cycle (The LPC).

Part 4: Clarifying Your Goals (Chapters 13-14), turns vision into direction. Chapter 13 helps you anchor in personal purpose, while Chapter 14 extends that clarity into the shared work of your team. Together they show how to balance enduring qualitative goals with evolving quantitative measures, align personal and team aspirations, and resolve contradictions that can quietly undermine progress.

Part 5 Conclusion: (Chapter 15), draws the threads together, showing how paradox-aware leadership is less a checklist than a lifelong practice. It invites you to return to your own context with clarity, courage, and tools for turning tension into trust, progress, and transformation.

This book has fresh insight, but it's all stuff we've known deep down for a long time. And desperately need to remember. Now.

So if you're tired of polarization—and perhaps tired of avoiding certain relatives during holiday dinners . . . if you're tired of shallow arguments, rigid thinking, and relationships strained by misunderstanding . . . if you're ready to move past feeling stuck, blocked, and frustrated in the pursuit of your goals . . .

This is for you.
This is for your team.
This is for the kind of leader the world needs now.

Welcome to paradox-aware leadership.

Part 1

The Basic Idea

Chapter 1

The Cost of Choosing Sides

The world I observe is one where polarization doesn't just shape headlines, it shapes our relationships, our workplaces, and even the way we view reality. Of course, this isn't new. History is full of moments when ideological battles escalated into family feuds, civil wars, or holiday dinners that ended in cold turkey and colder silence. But as I write, the speed, scale, and emotional intensity of these divisions feel uniquely overwhelming.

The Appeal and Cost of Polarization

It was a routine weekday morning when I had an unexpected call from the training director of a large library. A polarized fight about specific resources had become a fight about the funding of the whole institution. An uncomfortable pause in the call made it obvious what was at stake—jobs, community services, and archives that had outlasted generations. "We don't know whether the library will even exist next year," he said. I felt the resignation in his voice. I didn't know what to say, so I just listened. He didn't have much more to say, and the conversation ended awkwardly. The moment clarified something for me: Polarized leadership doesn't just wound combatants—it destroys adjacent things that seem innocent and unrelated.

Polarization can poison boardrooms, budgets, classrooms, and family text threads. It changes the way we plan, the way we relate, and the way we imagine the future. What once felt like healthy disagreement now feels like standing on opposite shores with no bridge in sight.

The quick appeal of polarized thinking is real. Ideological certainty feels like safety. It gives us clarity about who we are and where we stand—until that clarity starts doing damage.

US politics serve as an easily visible and widely impactful illustration. The zero-sum thinking of polarized leadership creates a kind of policy whiplash: One administration builds, the next tears down. This instability frustrates citizens, paralyzes public institutions, and makes private enterprise wary of long-term investment. When rules and regulations swing wildly with each election cycle, how do you build anything meant to last?

Polarized leadership causes problems far beyond the teams directly affected. With the US economy, the ripple effects are global. Domestic volatility becomes international turbulence. Allies hedge their bets. Trade partnerships stall. Global institutions are left guessing which version of America they're engaging this time. Meanwhile, trust in the democratic process itself erodes—not just in institutions, but between individual citizens.

And the human costs of polarized leadership run deep. Studies from the Pew Research Center show Americans are less likely to live near, marry, or even meaningfully engage with someone who holds opposing political beliefs. Political identity has become a new tribal boundary, outpacing even religion or race in determining where they live and who they trust. Polarized leadership turns what might have been a spirited exchange over dinner into a feud that could last generations.

Polarized leadership encourages people to sort themselves into literal or virtual enclaves based on ideology and identity. And when every challenge becomes a test of loyalty to your "side," nuance disappears, curiosity dries up, and leadership collapses into performance.

The Wisdom of the US Constitution

Ironically, the American political experiment is a powerful illustration of the cure as well as the disease. The founders of the American system anticipated the danger of polarized leadership. They didn't design their government to run smoothly under unanimity—they built it to function amid disagreement. The goal wasn't ideological purity. It wasn't dominance. It was durability. And they achieved that not by eliminating conflict, but by embedding it—structurally, intentionally, and with surprising philosophical foresight. If today's political climate feels like a pendulum swinging wildly between extremes, it's worth remembering that the original blueprint didn't fear tension. It relied on it.

In the sweltering summer of 1787, James Madison sat in Independence Hall scribbling feverishly. The air was thick. Philadelphia heat, wool coats, and powdered wigs didn't mix well, but Madison was focused on stakes higher than his own comfort. The American experiment was on the brink. The Articles of Confederation had failed. The union was fragile. The question before the delegates wasn't just how to govern—it was how to survive.

Madison didn't want a system that made winning easy. He wanted one that made domination hard.

They didn't design their government to run smoothly under unanimity—they built it to function amid disagreement.

Like many of the framers, he understood that the greatest threat to liberty wasn't chaos. It was concentrated power. And so, with deliberate genius, they embedded tension into the very architecture of American governance.

They didn't try to enshrine liberal or conservative values. They didn't codify a particular ideology. Instead, they designed a system to protect against the triumph of *any* single ideology. Through the separation of powers, federalism, staggered elections, and independent courts, they created a structure where opposing forces would constantly collide—productively.

They weren't idealists crafting a utopia. They were pragmatists channeling human nature. They expected disagreement. They planned for it. They believed that *out of that friction* would come refinement, accountability, and resilience. Progress, in their view, wasn't the product of dominance—it was the byproduct of tension.

It's not glamorous. It's not efficient. But it's brilliant.

This book shows how this kind of structural paradox fosters lasting innovation. It tempers extremes. It slows down bad ideas and forces better ones to emerge through debate, revision, and creative accommodation that doesn't dilute values but tests them.

It's worth asking: What would it mean to build our organizations, our teams, and our personal relationships with this same kind of resilient tension in mind?

Zero-Sum Thinking: The Enemy of Progress

Zero-sum thinking is the belief that for one side to win, the other must lose. It's the operating system of political pundits and playground bullies alike.

Paradox-aware leadership asks better questions: What if both sides are fighting *for* something good? What if each holds part of the truth? And what if sustainable solutions come not from silencing one voice, but from honoring the tension between them?

This doesn't mean compromise for compromise's sake. Paradox-awareness is not splitting the difference. It's not choosing the "middle way." It's about elevating the conversation—looking for a solution that integrates competing goods without diluting either one.

Zero-Sum in the Levant

In a Tel Aviv apartment, an Israeli mother clutches her phone, her face pale and blank. She's just learned that her kidnapped daughter is dead. On the Gaza side of the border, a Palestinian father kneels beside his daughter, who wakes in the night from dreams filled with drones.

They've never met. But they share a common grief—born from violence and the ideologies that feed it.

This is the cost of zero-sum leadership: a worldview in which one side's gain is automatically the other's loss. It's a mindset that has fueled decades of bloodshed, displacement, and despair. Again and again, polarized leaders have chosen narratives that demand the erasure of the other side's dignity, security, and claim to home. The result is not peace. It is paralysis—prolonged suffering with no true victors.

And yet, the most tragic irony lies in what both peoples know by experience: Genocide doesn't work. Not morally. Not strategically. Not practically. Jews and Muslims alike carry deep historical scars—legacies of persecution, exile, and state-sanctioned violence. They know what it means to be dehumanized. They know the cost of being seen as expendable. And still, when fear and ideology overpower empathy, history repeats itself.

A paradox-aware framework offers a different path. It begins when leaders recognize that the other side is fighting *for* something sacred—safety, identity, heritage, belonging. Paradox-aware leadership doesn't blend those values into bland compromise or false equivalency. Instead, it seeks a productive tension—a durable, protected, creative tension between competing goods.

In the midst of a conflict when stakes are high and emotions are raw, it's easy to stop seeing the other side as human. It's easy to believe leaders who flatten the other side into caricatures—villains, extremists, monsters. Leaders who do this trade reality for certainty. They give themselves moral permission to ignore, dismiss, or even destroy. Paradox-aware leadership offers a better way forward. It offers a better way of understanding what evil actually is.

Understanding Evil

Evil is what happens when a single good gets polarized—emphasized to the neglect of a counterbalancing good.

Paris, in June of 1794, provides a vivid example. In the Place de la Revolution and other public squares, the guillotine's blade glinted in the sun, rising and falling with grisly regularity. Crowds murmured as carts rolled in carrying nobles, peasants, and even fellow revolutionaries. All these were beheaded at the command of the Committee of Public Safety led by Maximilien Robespierre.

The committee had been formed in April of the year before in response to external and internal threats to the French Revolution. France was at war with a coalition of European powers and also faced counterrevolutionary revolts across the country. The committee was focused on two good things: justice for those who were oppressed under the prior regime, and safety from the powers that wanted to restore the former order.

The emphasis on justice and safety became polarized because they were not counterbalanced by mercy and due process. Justice became tyranny and safety hardened into the Reign of Terror. Robespierre said it this way: "Terror is nothing other than justice, prompt, severe, inflexible."

Understanding evil in this way helps us see how noble intentions can curdle. A hunger for justice becomes tyranny. A passion for truth becomes dogma. A drive for safety becomes oppression. And once we believe our good is *the only* good, we stop seeing people—and start labeling enemies.

Evil is what happens when a single good gets polarized— emphasized to the neglect of a counterbalancing good.

That's how well-meaning people end up supporting bullies and tyrants. That's how movements formed in defense of dignity turn into engines of exclusion. Evil doesn't always enter with malice. Sometimes, it walks in wearing our team colors.

To be clear: Some people *do* act with malice. There are manipulators. Sadists. People who enjoy harm. But even those dark impulses are often rooted in pain, fear, or warped self-protection. Paradox-awareness doesn't excuse the behavior—it explains its origin. And in doing so, it helps us resist evil—not by denying the overemphasized good and overreacting in the opposite direction, but by recognizing and also honoring the neglected good.

Paradox-awareness lets us separate people from their decisions. The same people who create harm with a polarized good can choose to also honor a counterbalancing good thing. Knowing that a person can make different choices is essential when you find that you have been causing harm with your own focus on one good thing and your neglect of something else that's also necessary. If you locate the evil in the person, you will have a hard time seeing your own need to change or believing that you, or anyone else, can change.

Seeing Ourselves in Polarized Leadership

Paradox-aware leadership invites you to change. Polarized leadership is something that exists, to varying degrees, in all of us. Sometimes it's in the way we lead teams, sometimes in the way we parent, sometimes in the way we carry unspoken expectations into our closest relationships.

The patterns are familiar. Leaders polarized toward **persistence** come across as stubborn, pushing a single course no matter the cost.

Leaders polarized toward **flexibility** can create chaos by constantly changing course and presenting confusing priorities. Leaders polarized toward **frankness** speak truth like a hammer, shattering trust instead of strengthening it. Leaders polarized toward **diplomacy** avoid hard conversations and give vague feedback, stalling progress and creating ambiguity.

The difficulty is that most leadership training fails polarized leaders. Why? Because our brains are wired in such a way that we mostly see only what we're looking for. If I'm overemphasizing accountability, I won't recognize or I'll choose to discount the absence of empathy because empathy contradicts what I'm fixated on. If I pride myself on persistence, I won't notice or won't care that inflexibility is exhausting my team.

Paradox-awareness gives us a way in. It starts by validating the good a problem leader is fighting for—whether that's results, justice, discipline, or clarity. From that shared ground, it's easier to open our eyes to the unwanted consequences that come from neglecting another good—flexibility, compassion, dignity, or trust.

This is why paradox-awareness is so powerful: it lets us see past the surface-level contradiction to the deeper pattern. It gives us confidence that there's always an innovative, nonobvious path forward that can honor both the strength we've been clinging to AND the good we've neglected. That shift—from defending one side to holding both—is often the moment leadership begins to heal.

Unwanted Consequences and the False Doctrine of Tradeoffs

Evil comes from neglecting something essential. When you are leading a team and getting unwanted results, you can be confident you are neglecting something important. As James Clear puts it in his book *Atomic Habits*: "Our lives are perfectly optimized for the results we are getting."

Polarized leaders resist this truth because they've embraced a false doctrine of inevitable tradeoffs: the zero-sum belief that we can only have one good at the expense of another. That warmth must come at the cost of truth-telling. That initiative requires the loss of cooperation. That self-confidence and openness to feedback can't coexist.

I want to clarify here that constraints are real—time, money, attention—all of these are limited resources. But within those constraints there are still an infinite number of possible paths. Geometry shows that through any fixed point, you can draw an infinite pencil of lines. There is always a way forward that honors both sides of a paradox. It will usually be creative and innovative, because it is by definition non-obvious, but it is there.

Choosing either/or is always a false choice. Polarized leadership is tempting because it may give short-term wins, but the neglected virtue will catch up in the end. Robespierre himself, who insisted that terror was nothing but "justice, prompt, severe, inflexible," eventually died by the same guillotine he had used to purge his opponents.

Paradox-aware leadership delivers breakthrough results. Most leaders, if they're honest, already suspect the source of their unwanted results. They know where they've neglected something important. What they don't see is the possibility of change, because they've believed the lie that necessary goods always come at another's expense.

But paradox-awareness exposes the lie. It helps us see that neglected goods can be reclaimed without sacrificing the ones we've already fought for. It shows us that progress doesn't come from abandoning discipline for compassion, or clarity for empathy, but from holding them together in creative tension.

That is the promise of paradox-aware leadership: Unwanted results are not dead ends. They are invitations. They point us back to what we've neglected and open a path to progress we couldn't see before.

Key Takeaways

- **Polarization offers false security.** The short-term clarity it promises eventually fractures teams, institutions, and relationships.
- **Evil is polarized good.** Justice without mercy, safety without due process, or truth without compassion curdle into tyranny, oppression, and dogma.

- **Polarization lives in all of us.** Overemphasizing one strength—persistence, frankness, accountability—while neglecting its counterpart creates unintended harm.
- **Paradox-awareness begins with validation.** Leaders can honor the good someone is fighting for while also naming the neglected counterpart that explains unwanted results.
- **Unwanted outcomes are diagnostic.** As James Clear reminds us, "Our lives are perfectly optimized for the results we are getting." If results are poor, something essential is being neglected.
- **Tradeoffs are not inevitable.** Constraints are real, but paradox-awareness shows there are always creative paths forward that honor both goods in tension.
- **Paradox-aware leadership is an invitation.** Unwanted results are not dead ends—they are signals that point us back to neglected goods and open possibilities for change.

CHAPTER 2

Embracing Productive Tension

Defining Paradox: The Ancient Thread
We've Forgotten

The last chapter showed how evil arises from a good intent taken too far. That observation about the way that opposites are entwined isn't something I thought up. You can find it in sacred texts, in moral philosophy, even in physics. Paradox is woven into the fabric of the universe.

Here are two illustrations from familiar physics:

1. A kite lifts into the sky when it catches the wind. The wind pulls and the string in your hand resists it. One day when my boys were young, we stood on an Oregon beach and cheered as our kite rose higher and higher, right out to the end of our string. "Let it go," they said. "Let it fly higher!" Of course, you know that it was the tension that kept it aloft. Release the tension, and it whips, it flutters, and eventually falls.

2. Gravity keeps us on the ground. It pulls us and the air in our atmosphere down toward the Earth. A jet engine creates thrust that runs perpendicular to gravity. Gravity provides downward force and the engine pushes against it. With those contradictory forces in play, the air moving over a wing shaped like an airfoil

creates a pressure difference that lifts an entire airplane off the ground. And so, the lift that takes us into the sky requires gravity.

A paradox is a seemingly self-contradictory proposition that, when investigated, turns out to be true. It is the tension that makes creation possible. It is the necessary friction that drives growth, insight, and moral progress.

In our rush for certainty, we've forgotten the sacred strain between opposites that gives life its meaning. We've built systems for efficiency, but not for wisdom. Our need for tidy answers has numbed us to the generative friction at the heart of every transformation.

The Bhagavad Gita, one of Hinduism's foundational scriptures, teaches that God is both within us and infinitely beyond us: "I am the Self . . . seated in the hearts of all creatures" (10:20). The divine is not *either* personal *or* cosmic—it is somehow *both*.

In Buddhist thinking, the *Heart Sutra* tells us that "form is emptiness, and emptiness is form"—a paradox that challenges us to release fixed definitions in order to see deeper truths.

In Islam, the Qur'an describes Allah as both "Most Merciful" and "severe in punishment"—a God of ultimate compassion *and* justice.

In Jewish wisdom literature, the writer of Ecclesiastes praises wisdom, and also says, "For in much wisdom is much grief, and he who increases knowledge increases sorrow." (1:18) Increased awareness includes painful realities like vanity, injustice, and the inevitability of death.

Here are three paradoxes from the New Testament (English Standard Version):

1. Jesus Christ was willing to endure the infinite agonies of the cross "for the joy that was set before him" (Hebrews 12:2).
2. "My grace is sufficient for you," says Christ, "for my power is made perfect in weakness" (2 Corinthians 12:9).
3. "For whoever would save his life will lose it, but whoever loses his life for my sake will find it" (Matthew 16:25).

Strength is made perfect in weakness. Life is found by losing it. These are not peripheral teachings. They are the very heart and basis of Christian discipleship.

In my own tradition, the Church of Jesus Christ of Latter-day Saints, Jesus Christ is the role model and the focus of worship precisely because he was tempted like everyone else and yet overcame. He has the power to save every soul because he innocently suffered the consequence of all human wrongdoing. As stated in the Doctrine and Covenants, He "ascended up on high, as also he descended below all things" (D&C 88:6).

The Book of Mormon teaches that "there is an opposition in all things," and goes so far as to say that without this opposition, "righteousness could not be brought to pass, neither wickedness, neither holiness nor misery, neither good nor bad" (2 Nephi 2:11). The opposition of contraries is, in other words, by divine design.

Across traditions—Hindu, Buddhist, Islamic, Jewish, Christian—the same truth echoes: Paradox is not a riddle to solve, but a reality to honor. It's not a barrier to human progression, but the means by which it happens.

Paradox is where the deepest truths live.

It's the universal pattern of transformation.

Our current practice of leadership is seldom informed by this knowledge. We settle instead for resolution, quick clarity, clean solutions. We've opted, as the Jedi master Yoda from the *Star Wars* movies would say, for the dark side of the force, because it is "quicker, easier, more seductive."

So paradox-awareness isn't a new idea. It's something we've known for a very long time. But it's something we have forgotten—especially in leadership. Our desire for certainty, for resolution, for control, has made us impatient with tension. We want simple choices, clear sides, silver-bullet solutions. And in doing so, we abandon the tension that could transform us. Tension is how people grow. It's how teams and organizations learn to thrive.

To become a paradox-aware leader is to learn to harness tension between contrary goods. To refuse false choices. To see the value in opposing truths. And to grow stronger, wiser, and more whole *because* of that tension—not in spite of it.

This chapter will begin to show you how.

Defining Paradox-Aware Leadership

You've been asked to cut costs *and* increase morale. Your team wants autonomy—but also clearer direction. You feel pressure to move fast—but know that patience will lead to better outcomes.

Sound familiar? These are paradoxes. And we would do well not to wish them away.

Paradox-aware leadership isn't about choosing sides. It's about standing in the space between them—with open eyes and a steady heart. It's leadership that dares to say: *Both are true, and neither can be ignored.*

A paradox is two essential truths, each valid, each pulling in different directions. And the tension between them is where the magic happens. Paradox-aware leaders don't seek to resolve these contradictions by eliminating one truth in favor of the other. Instead, they embrace and leverage this tension, creating balance, resilience, and innovation.

Here's the idea in a nutshell: The tension itself isn't the problem. It's actually key to the solution.

Think of it like breathing. Is it better to inhale or exhale? You'd never ask that, because the rhythm *The tension isn't in your way. It is the way.* of both is what sustains life. Paradox-aware leadership works the same way. Inhale decisiveness. Exhale collaboration. Inhale urgency. Exhale patience. It's this rhythm that gives teams oxygen.

The goal isn't to eliminate tension. It's to metabolize it—so your leadership becomes not just more balanced, but more deeply human. The tension isn't in your way. It *is* the way.

Spotting Everyday Paradoxes

So how do you spot paradoxes in your daily life or in the high-stakes decisions of leadership? It starts with expecting them. Once you realize that paradoxes are hiding in plain sight, you can proactively look for them.

You're in a meeting. Someone on your team wants to move fast. Someone else wants to gather more input. You feel torn. Decide quickly, or invite more voices? That torn feeling is the flag you're looking for. It signals to you that you're in a paradox. And if you can learn to see it, you can learn to lead through it.

You'll often find yourself leaning to one side or the other in situations like this. Learning to name the paradox, then, can help you identify realities you're neglecting and make better decisions more often.

Let's walk through how you might do that.

Step 1: Identify your own bias by asking yourself, *What would I advise someone else to do here?* Maybe: "Be bold. Decide."

Step 2: Determine a course of action aligned with that principle. Maybe: "Make the call. Take the lead."

Step 3: Now flip it. What's the opposite course of action? "Pause. Seek more feedback."

Step 4: And finally, ask yourself what principle or virtue would support that opposite action. "Be inclusive. Listen."

There it is—your paradox: decisiveness versus inclusiveness. Both grounded in a virtue. Both pulling on you. And both worth honoring. Being aware of the tension empowers you to act with greater nuance and effectiveness.

Examples of Paradox-Aware Leadership

April 1865. The American Civil War is ending. Lincoln stands at the edge of victory—and vengeance. Many of his contemporaries, including cabinet members, are urging him to impose justice with severe punishments on the South—proposals include mass confiscation of Southern property, extensive political disenfranchisement of Confederate leaders, and harsh military occupation to swiftly enact justice. Conversely, other advisors are advocating for policies of leniency, like immediate restoration of full political rights to former Confederates, minimal reparations, and rapid reintegration to foster healing and reconciliation.

Imagine, for a moment, you are Lincoln. What will you do?

Lincoln deeply valued both justice and compassion. He carefully navigated this tension with strategic decisions like the Emancipation Proclamation and his plan for Reconstruction, which balanced the imperative for justice with compassionate policies intended to reunite and heal the nation. His brilliance wasn't just in strategy—it was in restraint. With a fractured nation demanding both justice and mercy, he chose both. He freed the enslaved—and sought to heal the South. His paradox-aware leadership in this regard helped preserve the fragile union and set a course for unity and recovery after the war.

After decades of being imprisoned by the apartheid regime, Nelson Mandela had every reason to seek swift, decisive justice once elected president. But he understood the paradox between truth *and* reconciliation. Rather than fully pursuing either path exclusively, Mandela skillfully navigated both, establishing the Truth and Reconciliation Commission that acknowledged injustice but fostered national healing. His paradox-aware approach likely spared South Africa years of devastating internal conflict.

What if Lincoln had only chosen justice? The South might have buckled under occupation—but resentment would have simmered and reignited in the generations that followed.

What if Mandela had only chosen healing? The truth of apartheid might have been buried—and so would trust.

Paradox-aware leadership is an option for you just as it was for Lincoln and Mandela.

A Common Misconception

The US Civil War also offers a stark illustration of what paradox-aware leadership is *not*. It's not a lukewarm compromise. It's not conflict avoidance dressed up as consensus. It's not splitting the difference in a way that satisfies no one—and harms everyone.

I recently visited the National Portrait Gallery in Washington, DC, and stood several minutes contemplating the sharp angles in the face of Henry Clay. Henry Clay was Speaker of the House of Representatives in the decades before the Civil War. He understood the arguments of the abolitionists in the North. He also understood the claims to property rights and self-determination from the South. He could hear the rhetoric of division getting sharper, feel the friction escalating, and the likelihood of a rupture growing. More than anything, he wanted to avoid bloodshed. He proposed, and managed to pass, the Missouri

Compromise—a piece of legislation that fixed the legality and illegality of slavery along defined borders.

Henry Clay was a moderate who understood both sides of a tension, so It's tempting to think of him as a paradox-aware leader. He wasn't. His grand compromise solution split the difference and honored neither side fully. It perpetuated a fundamental injustice by allowing slavery to continue. It also failed to secure the fundamental investment and property rights of Southerners.

A paradox-aware solution would have had to do the unthinkable: Eliminate slavery *and* honor the property rights of slaveholders.

"Impossible," you might say.

Seemingly impossible, I counter.

Because this is where paradox does its fiercest work—not by asking us to choose between truths, but by forcing us to imagine solutions no one has seen before.

Paradox-aware solutions are always unexpected and new, because they are fitted to the specifics of a time, a place, and the people involved. So it may be impossible to say, from our present vantage point, exactly what a paradox-aware solution to the slavery question would have looked like, but the following facts may stretch your imagination:

1. **Fact 1:** Economists Daron Acemoglu and James A. Robinson won a Nobel Prize for showing how economies that empower people at the lowest levels—local ownership, decentralized decision-making—tend to outperform command-and-control systems by orders of magnitude. Their work demonstrates that a thousand acres of rich southern farmland worked by 20 informed (educated) stewards making autonomous and coordinated decisions and who stand to benefit from their own labor will generate more wealth than 20 enslaved people working the same land ever could.

2. **Fact 2:** Economic historians Claudia Goldin and Frank Lewis determined that the North and South spent a combined $7 billion (in 1860 dollars) just in direct costs. That doesn't begin to factor in losses from property damage, trade disruption, and 1.5 million casualties. By contrast, the estimated total economic value of four million enslaved people in 1860 was under $4

billion. Even the most generous emancipation compensation scheme would have been cheaper—and far more humane—than the war the United States chose instead.

Paradox-aware leadership doesn't settle for stalemates. It demands courage, creativity, and a willingness to honor both sides of a paradox—especially when conventional wisdom insists that you can't.

The search for paradox-aware solutions is an act of faith. By definition, such solutions are not immediately visible. You choose to search for them because you choose to believe they are out there. Others have found them before. With practice, you'll know you can find them yourself. But in every fresh circumstance, you must choose to seek again.

> *The search for paradox-aware solutions is an act of faith. By definition, such solutions are not immediately visible. You choose to search for them because you choose to believe they are out there.*

Your Paradox Toolkit

Spotting paradoxes becomes easier and more intuitive the more you practice. Beyond the initial four-step exercise described earlier, here are a few more ways to harness paradox effectively:

- **Both/And Thinking:** Train yourself to replace "either/or" with "both/and." This subtle shift encourages your brain to hold two truths simultaneously, fostering creative solutions rather than forced compromises.
- **Identify Core Values and Goals:** Clarify and articulate the core values underlying your decisions and what you're fundamentally trying to accomplish. Often, paradoxes emerge from tensions between equally valid values, like innovation versus reliability or transparency versus discretion. Recognizing these values upfront helps you navigate the tensions thoughtfully.
- **Pause for Paradox:** In decision-making meetings, briefly pause discussions to explicitly name tensions rather than rush to

quick resolutions. This practice deepens organizational insight and opens pathways to innovative solutions.

Remember, paradox-aware leadership isn't a passive approach. It requires courage, humility, and patience. It means not having all the answers immediately and staying open to refining your understanding. But paradox-aware leaders aren't intimidated by complexity—they thrive in it.

Welcome to the adventure of paradox-aware leadership, where tensions aren't obstacles but invitations to deeper insight, richer relationships, and more powerful results. Embracing paradox is like riding a bike—initially awkward and occasionally wobbling. But once you find your balance, it becomes second nature, exhilarating, and empowering.

Paradox-aware leadership isn't an epiphany or a one-time a shift in mindset—it's a discipline you develop through practice. That's what the next seven chapters do. Each one explores a specific leadership tension: strength and vulnerability, confidence and caution, flexibility and grit, and more. These aren't sterile ideas—they're the emotional crossroads you'll face in hard conversations, high-stakes decisions, and everyday interactions.

As you engage with each tension, you'll begin to recognize the familiar shape of paradox in your own life. You'll start to feel the rhythm of "both/and" in your gut, not just your mind. And over time, you'll build the kind of leadership presence that's resilient, wise, and deeply human.

So take a breath. Let the tension come. You're not alone—and you're only racing against yourself.

Key Takeaways

- **Paradox is foundational.** From scripture to science, it's clear that life, growth, and wisdom depend on tension between opposing truths.
- **Every tradition honors paradox.** Whether it's Christ's strength in weakness, the Bhagavad Gita's union of internal and cosmic divinity, or the Qur'an's pairing of mercy and justice—paradox is a thread that runs through all sacred understanding.

- **Paradox-aware leadership is intentional tension.** Instead of choosing sides, great leaders hold space for competing truths, honoring both while searching for creative, durable solutions.
- **You'll know you're in a paradox when you feel torn.** That discomfort—especially in high-stakes moments—is not a bug in your leadership. It's a flag signaling that the moment requires deeper wisdom.
- **Paradox-aware solutions are never "split-the-difference" compromises.** They are bold, surprising, and context-specific—found only when we believe they're possible and are willing to search.
- **The tension is the way forward.** Learning to lead through paradox doesn't simplify your work—it deepens it. And it makes you the kind of leader your best future needs.

Part 2

**Everyday Paradoxes
in Leadership
(Practical Examples)**

CHAPTER **3**

Strength and Vulnerability in Leadership

Y ou're standing in front of your team after a project tanks. The room is quiet. Everyone's looking at you. I've certainly lived that moment—multiple times—when my bold new growth initiative just didn't deliver. Part of you wants to say, "Here's what went wrong, and I'll fix it." Strong. Certain. In control. The other part wants to say, "I don't have all the answers right now. And that scares me too." Vulnerable. Human. You feel caught between strength and vulnerability—and are afraid that choosing either will cost you credibility.

Which way will you go? Do you instinctively lean to one side? Conventional wisdom gives us mixed messages:

- "Never let them see you sweat"—but also "Be real."
- "Be decisive"—but also "Use emotional intelligence."

Maybe you try to split the difference—speak with authority, but keep it real. Be authentic, but, please, not too messy. Your results may initially look like a lot of uncomfortable silence during team check-ins and emails that somehow feel like therapy transcripts and press releases at the same time.

I worked under a vice president once who specialized in certainty—bold, uninformed, unjustified, certainty. His credibility lasted exactly as long as it took the team to see he didn't know what he was talking about. I worked with another leader who continually emphasized his own limitations. He was easy to like, but hard to follow sometimes.

If you've felt this tension, you're not alone. So here's the good news: This isn't a problem you need to solve. It's a paradox you're meant to live in. Because strength and vulnerability aren't opposites. They're partners. And learning to lead with both will change everything.

The False Dilemma of Strength Versus Vulnerability

You may have seen Emanuel Leutze's painting of George Washington crossing the Delaware River on a desperate December night. He's standing upright in a rowboat, icy wind lashing his coat, eyes fixed on the far shore. He looks unshakable. But inside? He knows the river is freezing, the outcome is uncertain, and the lives of his men hang in the balance. What the painting doesn't show is the storm within.

You may have also seen a YouTube video featuring Brené Brown, microphone in hand, talking about shame, courage, and the power of saying, "I don't know." She makes the case for a rather different vision of leadership—one that says vulnerability isn't weakness. It's *where courage begins.*

One moment you may want to be like Washington—stoic, resolute, invincible. The next you may believe that the key to trust is vulnerability, even tears. Perhaps you've tried to reconcile the two—and ended up wondering if you're failing at both.

Maybe the problem isn't the advice. Maybe it's the question. What if strength and vulnerability weren't opposite ends of a spectrum? What if they were partners in the same brave dance?

Entering the Paradox

This is the part where your brain starts to push back. It wants clarity, not contradiction. It wants a clear path, not two competing instincts. But paradox-aware leadership doesn't work that way. Instead of solving the tension, you live in it. Strength and vulnerability are like inhaling and exhaling. One draws power in; the other lets it move through. One without the other is suffocation. Together, they're life.

We have no film that captures the moment, but if you close your eyes, you can imagine Churchill at a microphone in 1940. Britain has just lost thousands of men in France and narrowly escaped annihilation on the beaches of Dunkirk. His citizenry, and the whole world, is watching. He begins with grim honesty: "The whole root and core and brain of the British Army . . . has been thrown back." He doesn't hide the losses. He doesn't fake optimism. He names the loss. The pain. The fear. And then, from that ground of truth, he rises: "We shall fight on the beaches, we shall fight on the landing grounds, we shall fight in the fields and in the streets, we shall fight in the hills; we shall never surrender." That line was forged in the fire of vulnerability. That's what made it believable. That's what made it powerful.

Even if you're not as eloquent as Churchill, you have the power to stay present—long enough to see that strength and vulnerability don't cancel each other out. They *complete* each other.

Recognizing the Tension in Your Own Leadership

Search your own history for a hard moment—a tough conversation, a failing project, a disappointed team. Part of you wants to show up strong: Deliver the plan, hold your ground, keep things moving. Another part wants to admit how hard this is, to say: "I'm not sure either." And right there—in that pause—is the paradox asking to be seen.

I have a memory of an experience with exactly this tension. It was during an annual planning meeting where I had to report on our progress with an adjacent market we'd invested in that year. The returns were a small fraction of the investment. The team needed direction for the coming year, but I didn't feel like I understood the situation well enough to even explain why we had failed.

Most of us lean one way or the other by default. Maybe you're the steady hand—always composed, rarely rattled. Maybe you're the open soul—always honest, rarely hidden. Neither is wrong. But both, by themselves, have blind spots.

Strength without vulnerability can isolate. Vulnerability without strength can unsettle. But when you combine the two? That's when trust forms. That's when people lean in.

So pay attention to your instinct. It's not your enemy—it's your starting point. And next time you feel pulled one way, ask yourself:

- *How could vulnerability make me more trustworthy here?*
- *How could strength give this moment more clarity and calm?*

Paradox-aware leadership isn't about being perfect. It's about being present—with the full range of what this moment needs.

Paradox in Practice: Finding the Balance

So what does it actually look like to lead with both strength and vulnerability? To hold power without losing softness—and to show your heart without losing command?

Consider Oprah Winfrey, someone I've come to deeply admire. For decades, she's invited the world into conversations about trauma, hope, and healing. Her vulnerability is unmistakable. She has cried with guests, shared her own pain, opened space for others to be real. But beneath that openness is steel. Clear vision. High standards. A media empire built not just on kindness but excellence. Her strength doesn't cancel her vulnerability. It's what gives it credibility.

Michael Jordan is another imperfect but instructive example, one that's fascinated me as a basketball fan for a long time. Ruthlessly competitive. He pushed himself and others to the brink. He wanted greatness—and demanded it from himself and his teammates. But in moments that mattered, he also showed the cracks: honoring his coaches, admitting his limits, showing raw emotion. That's what made him more than a machine. That's what connected him to his teammates.

Strength and vulnerability don't dilute each other. They give each other meaning. Oprah and Jordan aren't superhuman exceptions; they each had their predispositions as starting places. But they are reminders that the best leaders *feel* the full range—and dare to lead from it. You don't need to be superhuman. You just need to stop pretending strength and vulnerability can't live in the same room.

Facing Resistance

Let's be honest. This sounds hard.

Balance strength and vulnerability? In real time? With real people? In a real workplace that's moving fast and breaking things? Wouldn't it be easier to just pick a lane and stay there? Easier? Sure. But far less effective.

General George Washington didn't lead from a single playbook. He led with a responsive and attuned human presence. In the winter of 1777, the Revolutionary War looked unwinnable for the Americans. At Valley Forge, Washington's men were starving, freezing, and deserting. He didn't bark orders or give fiery speeches. He walked quietly among them, asking questions, listening, and feeling the same chill wind they did. He also drilled them with new discipline learned from a Prussian commander, Baron von Steuben. Back in his tent, Washington wrote letter after desperate letter begging for supplies. Stoic strength. Quiet vulnerability. Both, at once.

By 1783, the war was all but won and those faithful soldiers felt betrayed—they had bled and died, but Congress hadn't paid them. Whispers spread of a coup against Congress. General Washington heard about it and called a meeting with his officers in Newburgh, New York. Instead of matching their treason with threats or punishment, Washington was measured and composed. At one point, he fumbled for his reading glasses because he couldn't see the small print on a letter he was trying to read to them. He famously said, "Gentlemen, you must pardon me. I have grown gray in your service and now find myself growing blind."

In the accounts of those present, that one soft, human, and unguarded sentence was a tipping point in the mood of the officers. Some were moved to tears as they considered his living example of self-sacrifice. They abandoned the conspiracy and remained loyal to the Constitution. In that pivotal moment in the meeting with his officers, it was his admission of weakness that created an emotional connection and turned the flow of history.

I've never stopped a coup, but I've had moments where the only thing that turned the room was honesty.

Embracing Your Journey

If you're feeling unsure right now—good. That means you're in the doorway. Leadership isn't about flawless execution. It's about courageous presence. Staying with the discomfort long enough to let it shape you into something wiser.

That's what Washington did. He didn't have all the answers, but he showed up, again and again, with integrity and humanity. He commanded a revolution and embodied the paradox that kept it from falling apart.

As you begin to do the same, something inside you will change. You'll start noticing the subtle signals—when your team needs strength, when they need softness, when they need both. You'll stop reaching for one right answer and start leading from a deeper intuition.

And when you do, your presence will shift the room. Paradox-aware leadership inspires confidence *and* invites connection. It earns respect *and* builds love.

This is what happens when you stop choosing sides or splitting the difference, and instead get intentional about finding the balance. Welcome to the practice.

Key Takeaways

- **Strength and vulnerability are partners.** Great leaders don't toggle between them; they learn to lead from both at once.
- **Trying to "split the difference" between strength and vulnerability often creates confusion.** Integration is more effective than dilution.
- **You likely have a default posture.** Some lean toward strength, others toward vulnerability. Both have blind spots. Paradox-aware leaders learn to stretch into the side they usually avoid.
- **Trust forms when people see both your steadiness and your humanness.** Vulnerability invites connection. Strength creates safety. You need both to lead well.
- **Paradox-aware leadership is about staying present in contradictions.** The tension is uncomfortable, but it's also where growth, trust, and transformation happen.

CHAPTER 4

Caution Versus Confidence

You're at a crossroads. A bold idea is on the table—uncharted, risky, potentially game-changing.

One voice inside you says, *Go.* Another voice says, *Not yet.*

Your team is watching. The clock is ticking. In this moment, leadership feels like standing on the edge of a high dive—do you leap, or do you climb down and measure the depth again?

Confidence says: *Jump.* Caution says: *Check again.* Which will you choose?

That feeling of paralysis—when you're too anxious to leap but too restless to stay put—is a clue that a paradox is pressing in. Stuckness isn't failure, it's the invitation to notice the tension and step into it with awareness.

The Seductive Appeal of Boldness

Antarctica, 1914. A ship called *Endurance* has become trapped, frozen solid in a sea of ice. Supplies are running low. The 27-man crew is stranded with no hope of rescue. The captain has to decide whether to stay with the relative stability of the still-intact ship or launch a lifeboat into an open, freezing ocean—navigating hundreds of miles through deadly seas to try to reach a supply outpost. That captain was Ernest Shackleton. He chose to take the gamble on the open sea. Against all odds, every one of his men survived.

We make movies about stories like this. Boldness is electric. It moves fast. It sounds like: *We'll build the plane while flying.*

Maybe your leadership doesn't take you through polar blizzards. But you will face moments that offer you a leap of faith: to launch the new product, change the strategy, say yes before you feel ready. And you know that if it works, you'll become a legend.

But you also know that these stories don't always end well. Courage isn't always rewarded with miraculous success.

The Quiet Power of Caution

Where Shackleton navigated disaster, another polar explorer quietly redefined success. Roald Amundsen made history with preparation. Before leading the first expedition to reach the South Pole, he spent years studying native Arctic survival techniques. He used sled dogs and skis and wore Inuit-style furred skins instead of woolen overcoats. He practiced meticulously and mapped every contingency by establishing a chain of supply depots on his route to the pole.

There was still risk and they still encountered setbacks, but as early 20th century polar expeditions go, Amundsen's trip to the South Pole was stable and uneventful. It's true that they ate some of the sled dogs, but then, that had always been part of the plan. Not much drama and nobody ever made a movie about it.

So ask yourself which style speaks to you. Do you resonate with the daring of Shackleton or the discipline of Amundsen? Both have their place. No lasting success is possible without a healthy measure of each. I've often found myself drawn to the Shackleton archetype— the quick-moving, high-stakes decision-maker. But the older I get, the more I admire Amundsen's brand of quiet competence. His success didn't make headlines, but it saved lives. That kind of leadership has a quieter kind of power—and sometimes a deeper one.

Discovering Your Own Leadership Balance

Here's where the stories stop being about explorers—and start being about you. What would it mean for you to lead with both confidence and caution?

Maybe that question feels threatening. Maybe you've built success to this point on your boldness—or your restraint. Why dilute that?

Here's the key that paradox-aware leaders understand: The tension between them doesn't sap your strength. It expands it.

Confidence without caution is recklessness. Caution without confidence is hesitation. But if you lean into the tension, you get movement with mindfulness. Vision with precision. Paradox-aware leadership builds the capacity to embrace both.

Facing Your Own Leadership Paradox

So imagine yourself in a meeting with your own team. You're facing a choice between a path that feels fast and risky, and another that feels slow and safe. All eyes are on you. This is a moment that reveals your leadership reflex. Do you instinctively reach for bold action? Or do you start scanning for risks?

I remember once fast-tracking a project based on a hunch. It felt right in the moment—bold, decisive, even inspiring. Three weeks later, we had to walk it back because I hadn't paused to ask whether the systems were in place to support it. That moment taught me that boldness without groundwork can create confusion, not momentum.

Neither is wrong. But both, by themselves, have blind spots. And the more aware you are of your own default, the more power you have to lead with intention.

So try this:

- If your instinct is to *move fast,* pause and ask: *What risks am I overlooking—and who can help me see them?*
- If your instinct is to *play it safe,* ask: *What bold opportunity am I deferring—and what might it cost to wait?*

Paradox-aware leadership doesn't mean you'll always get it right. Instead, it just helps you notice when you're off balance—and lets you choose to move toward wholeness.

The Worth of a Counterweight Colleague

So the next time you're excited by a bold idea, the timing feels right, and your gut says *go*, look for that teammate who says, "Let's model three downside scenarios first." You may sigh, or even chafe, but deep down, you know they're probably saving you from a mistake.

Great leaders don't just tolerate tension, they *invite* it. Especially from the people who challenge their defaults.

Some of us never met a risk we didn't love. Others can't imagine moving forward without a spreadsheet, a backup plan, and a meeting to debrief the backup plan.

The best leadership teams don't eliminate those differences, they leverage them. Bold leaders need cautious voices to slow them down when the edge is near. Cautious leaders need bold partners to say, "Yes, it's risky—but it's time."

So ask yourself: *Who pushes me to think differently? And when they do, do I resent them, or do I lean in?*

For many years, my business partner, Jeromy, played that role for me. When I was the one saying, "Nothing happens till you burn the boats!" He was the one asking, "Have we thought through contingencies?" The plans that emerged from the tension were sharper than what either of us would have followed alone. Every leader needs someone like that.

The Ordeal: Navigating Real-World Complexity

Every leader faces a moment of reckoning—when confidence alone won't carry you, and caution can't protect you. That's the ordeal. And how you move through it reveals everything.

In 1997, Steve Jobs returned to a floundering Apple. The brand was bloated. The vision was muddy. His move? Slash the product line by 70 percent. It looked bold, and it was. But it was also deeply deliberate. Jobs had spent months studying the market, listening to customers, and refining what mattered. His boldness was born from focus, not bravado.

Satya Nadella stepped into Microsoft's top job with less fanfare, but no less audacity. With a calm voice and a listening posture, he began reshaping the company's future: cloud-first, AI-forward, culture-centered. His caution created trust. His confidence created change.

We all face these crossroads—maybe not on a global stage, but in boardrooms, team meetings, even one-on-one check-ins. I've had to make those calls with limited data, knowing that every path had risk. What I've learned is that the tension doesn't go away. But with practice, it becomes familiar. And eventually, it becomes a source of strength.

These aren't contradictions. They're catalysts. Paradox-aware leadership doesn't live at the extremes. It lives in the dynamic tension between clarity and risk, steadiness and speed. And when you learn that rhythm, the impossible becomes possible.

Leading with Balanced Wisdom

Imagine now what it will look like for you to set a bold vision and back it with a steady, thoughtful plan. How will you lead your team through uncertainty, with the courage to act and the wisdom to listen? That becomes your style when you stop seeing confidence and caution as rivals, and start seeing them as teammates.

Caution looks ahead for danger. Confidence looks ahead for opportunity. Paradox-aware leadership looks ahead—and brings both.

So where might you pause this week? Where might you push forward?

Paradox-aware leadership doesn't ask you to mute your instincts. It asks you to tune them—to listen for the harmony between boldness and care. You don't have to choose between being careful and courageous. You were born to be both.

Key Takeaways

- **Confidence and caution are allies.** When held in tension, they create movement with mindfulness and ambition with accountability.
- **Boldness is inspiring.** Stories like Shackleton's remind us that courageous leaps must still account for real risks.

- **Caution is wisdom.** Amundsen's meticulous planning saved lives and proved that slow and steady leadership is just as heroic.
- **Your leadership reflex matters.** Whether your instinct is to leap or to linger, awareness of your default gives you the power to lead with intention, not impulse.
- **Paradox-aware leaders ask different questions.** They pause to consider the overlooked risks—or the hidden costs of waiting too long.
- **Trust the tension between teammates.** The voices that slow you down—or push you forward—may be your most valuable leadership assets.
- **You don't have to mute your instincts—just tune them.** Courage and caution can coexist, and when they do, they create a leadership style that's both visionary and grounded.

CHAPTER 5

Personal Goals Versus Team Goals in Leadership

I t's Monday morning. The team's on Zoom. Everyone nods as you walk through the quarterly targets. Smiles all around. "Sounds great," they say. But one person is secretly planning a Himalayan trek. Another is sketching ideas for a yoga studio. Someone else has been playing jazz saxophone gigs in nightclubs and is quietly hoping to make a career of it.

Everyone's in the meeting. But not everyone's *in* the meeting.

We all do this. We show up. We nod at the team goals. We're committed to doing our part, but behind the scenes, we're chasing our own meaning in a dozen directions. I've smiled through planning meetings with a part of my brain quietly sketching out ideas for a new app I was building after hours. I wasn't disengaged—I was just also engaged, emotionally and mentally, in other things.

The workplace assumption for most of my working life is that if you have personal ambitions that are separate from work, you should keep them to yourself. Fine if you have them, but don't let them interfere with your work. It makes sense. If you're being paid to do a job, you should do that job, not something else.

Over time, I've come to understand that honoring those personal sparks isn't a threat to team momentum. It's actually essential to real alignment.

Paradox-aware leaders don't demand that team members segregate personal dreams from their work. They find a way to *incorporate* them— and still move the team forward. That's what this chapter is about.

The Great Misunderstanding

A new leader steps in, fresh with strategy decks and a crisp vision. "Let's align," she says. "No personal agendas. Just the mission." Everyone nods. Goals are shared. Dashboards light up.

But beneath it all, one person's plotting an exit. Another's chasing a certification they've never mentioned. A third is quietly burned out and dreaming of a sabbatical.

There is among too many leaders a great misunderstanding: that personal goals don't matter when you're focused on team goals. They actually do.

Ignoring personal aspirations is like ignoring gravity. You can pretend it's not there—but eventually, something's going to fall. And leaders who pretend people are blank slates with job titles don't build trust. They build turnover.

If you've ever felt frustrated trying to move a team forward while honoring individual needs, you've been caught in a paradox. The frustration itself is a signal: You're not failing, you're being invited to notice and name the paradox at play.

If you want alignment that lasts, you start by acknowledging what's already pulling on your team.

The Hidden Power of Personal Goals

Here's a twist to consider: The best way to build team success may be to stop focusing only on the team.

In a mastermind group, I met a man named Sam Bradford. Sam started out as a youth pastor—idealistic, passionate, ready to serve. But a dysfunctional organizational culture left him burnt out and looking for a change. He took a job as a barista at Dutch Bros Coffee. Just something temporary to pay the bills. But what he found there was unexpected.

Dutch Bros didn't just ask for performance. They asked about purpose. His manager wanted to know what Sam *dreamed* about. What he *hoped* to become. That question changed everything. Relatively quickly, Sam found an outlet for his ministering fire as the head of people development at Dutch Bros—a company where the hiring sign doesn't say, "Help Wanted." It says, "Leaders Built Here." Sam was responsible for helping the mostly young employees chart a vision for their future far beyond Dutch Bros.

What I love about this story is how it flips the script on the relationship between work and life. The theory is that when the mostly young and transient baristas see work at Dutch Bros on the critical path to their own life goals, they will do better work for as long as they stay. It works. They tend to love on customers in the same way they feel loved. And they tend to stay much longer than the industry average.

So I've tried to ask those same kinds of questions in my own teams—and I've seen how they unlock energy I didn't know was there.

Balancing Individual and Collective Success

You might be thinking: *This sounds like a nice sentiment. But we've got goals to hit and real deadlines. Aren't personal dreams a distraction?*

It's a fair concern. The data on this question suggests something intriguing. When leaders support personal aspirations, people don't disengage—they dig in. They stop working for approval and start working with ownership. It turns out that people are inherently motivated by more than paychecks or praise. They're most powerfully motivated by meaning, fulfillment, and personal achievement.

Research on transformational leadership shows that when leaders tap into deeper chords of meaning and provide ways for people to experience personal fulfillment:

- Motivation goes up.
- Creativity goes up.
- Engagement skyrockets—especially when people feel they can make real decisions, build their individual competence, and enjoy satisfying relationships.

Research in self-determination theory confirms that engagement is highest when a work environment supports three basic human needs:

1. Autonomy—a feeling of ownership of your actions and choices
2. Competence—a feeling of being effective and capable
3. Relatedness—a feeling of connection to others in caring relationships

These conditions are the trifecta of employee engagement and satisfaction. The more you support the person, the stronger the team becomes. That's not idealism. That's leadership tuned to how humans actually work.

Personal Goals Versus Internal Politics

Suppose a team member volunteers to lead a high-visibility project. And quietly, you wonder: *Is this initiative about the mission—or their résumé?*

I know I'm not the only one who has worried that encouraging personal aspirations might accidentally open the door to hidden agendas—that supporting personal goals could open the floodgates to selfish personal fiefdoms and maybe even backroom maneuvering.

So let me be clear: Personal goals are not the same as private agendas. Private agendas are comparative and competitive in nature. Personal goals are possible without reference to anyone else. Personal goals can be open. They can be shared, and they create interpersonal connections. Private agendas are, by definition, hidden. They create suspicion. When we talk more about goals in a later chapter I'll come back to this, but for now, I'll just say that internal politics can't survive in environments with shared purpose and clarity. They thrive in silence, ambiguity, and mistrust.

When leaders name the team vision clearly, and invite team members to name their dreams too, alignment gets easier, not harder. Transparency doesn't invite dysfunction. It disarms it.

Handling Personal Goals Respectfully

You want to understand your team members. What drives them? What matters to them? In asking those questions, you may also hear a voice in your head that says: *What if I intrude on something too personal? What if this gets weird?*

That's valid. Personal goals often touch vulnerable places—health, family, spirituality, identity. And that's why care and consent matter.

The goal isn't to collect data, it's to build trust. Ask with openness. Receive with humility. Never push. Never pry. Paradox-aware solutions are invitations, not mandates. People choose them because they are a better way forward. They don't require coercion.

Paradox-aware solutions are invitations, not mandates.

Also, legal protections like HIPAA, ADA, and GDPR exist for a reason. Paradox-aware leaders aren't driven by compliance—they build cultures where people feel emotionally safe before they're ever asked to share.

So start small. Offer your own goals first. Ask, "Is there something inside or outside of work you'd love to grow in this year?" If they engage, great. If they pass, that has to be OK too. Trust only grows where people feel free to choose.

Practical Tools for the Journey

One afternoon, a team member mentions she's training for a marathon. You nod, smile—and remember. A few weeks later, you ask how the training is coming along. She lights up.

I once had a teammate mention that she was planning for a 10-day intensive meditation retreat. I asked about what it meant to her, how we could support it, and later, how it had gone. In each interaction, I could see the shift in her posture, her smile—it reminded me how powerful it is to simply notice.

Moments like this can matter more than you might expect. Because you aren't just tracking tasks. You're seeing a life in motion. Supporting personal goals doesn't require scheduling a formal meeting specifically for that purpose. It can simply mean weaving curiosity into how you lead—consistently and sincerely.

Try this:

- Create space for one-on-one conversations that go beyond status updates.
- Ask about what they're working toward—at work or outside of it.
- Look for sparks: what excites them, what challenges they've chosen.
- When you notice alignment, name it. Offer a project, a role, a moment.
- And when the goals aren't work-related? Show up anyway—with encouragement, not evaluation.

Sometimes, the greatest leadership act isn't solving a problem. It's simply saying, "I see you."

The Power of Integrative Leadership

Imagine leading a team where people show up with more than skills and experience. They bring their hopes. Their strengths. Their purpose.

One person lights up to mentoring new hires—because teaching energizes them. Another finds unexpected joy in leading client calls—because storytelling is their craft. They're not just executing tasks. They're channeling the best version of themselves into what they do.

When leaders share their own goals first—whether it's finishing their novel, running a half-marathon, or learning to parent better—it creates a ripple. It raises the room's humanity. It says: "You don't have to disappear to belong."

Integration isn't idealism. It's how trust scales. It's how teams move from transactional to transformational. And it starts with your choice to lead as a whole person.

If at First You Don't Succeed . . .

Paradox-aware leadership is a bit like juggling. You learn to do it with practice. The goal isn't to reduce the number of balls. It's to grow your skill at keeping them moving.

I once asked a colleague who was making a great contribution as a part-time employee whether she was interested in going full time. I found out indirectly that this conversation had triggered concerns that her schedule wasn't matching the needs of the business. I intended my question as a compliment, but I didn't know that full time was a bad fit for her commitments as a mom. Luckily, I was able to circle back and clarify. But I learned that just because I think I'm being appreciative and supportive doesn't mean everyone else will hear what I say in that light.

Learning to honor both personal and professional commitments may sometimes feel messy. You may drop balls and miss beats. But with a little persistence and humility, over time you find the rhythm: Support personal dreams, align team goals, hold both with grace.

That's the simple truth: You don't need to pick. You need to practice.

Key Takeaways

- **Team alignment doesn't erase personal ambition.** People show up with dreams, doubts, and side projects—even if they don't say them out loud.
- **Ignoring personal goals breeds turnover.** People who feel unseen will eventually go looking for meaning elsewhere.
- **Supporting personal goals strengthens team performance.** When people feel known, they engage more deeply and contribute with ownership.
- **Private agendas and personal goals are not the same.** One hides in silence; the other thrives in transparency.
- **Great leaders create space for the human behind the role.** They listen with care, ask without prying, and lead with consent, not coercion.
- **You don't need a strategy document to start.** A well-timed question, a remembered detail, or a moment of sincere curiosity is often enough to unlock connection.

Chapter 6

Measurable Versus Qualitative Goals

Profits were solid, stock options were trending up, and my team—a small one within a big company—was on track to hit our release date. Judging by metrics, everything looked great. But something was off.

No one could quite explain how our work fit into the company's bigger picture. The vibe on the team was . . . wary. Like we were all waiting for someone to say what we were really doing. Somehow, we were checking every box—and still feeling like extras in an episode of *The Office*. When the day of downsizing finally came and most of us were, in fact, laid off, that "off" vibe was vindicated.

The time I spent on that team taught me something: The numbers can say you're thriving while your gut whispers a deeper truth—you're drifting. That's the paradox at the heart of this chapter: We measure what we can see—but we're driven by what we feel.

There have been times when I've obsessed over tracking deliverables with perfect precision. I've gloried in Gantt charts on top of spreadsheets. But over time, I've noticed that when my team was most motivated, it wasn't because the metrics were sharp—it was because the purpose was clear.

Paradox-aware leadership means learning to live in that tension—without reducing it. Metrics give structure. Purpose gives soul. And without both, a team doesn't move forward. It just spins.

The Pitfalls of Neglect

Whenever you neglect either qualitative or the quantitative goals, you get weak results. A little imagining may be helpful here:

Imagine a fired-up leader who is done with mediocrity and wants to raise the bar. She writes, "Be the best at what we do" on the whiteboard. Everyone nods. But no one knows what to do next. *What exactly do we do? For whom? By when?* The vagueness feels lofty—but lands like fog. You can't steer in it. She's neglected to provide any measurable targets.

Imagine another manager who has heard too many customer complaints about feeling ignored and decides to start tracking email response time down to the minute. What gets measured gets better, and before long the response time trend looks impressive. Progress seems provable. But to hit those numbers, the team is avoiding or glossing over complex customer issues because . . . they slow the response time average. They got that speed—but they're still frustrating customers.

I can't resist one more example because I've seen it so often. It starts with a manager who believes, almost religiously, in the virtue of hard work. The team gets it. Everyone's busy. Calendars are full. Metrics are moving. But no one asks: "Are we actually making progress?" It's the organizational version of jogging in place—exhausting, but you haven't gone anywhere.

You've probably lived in situations like these. Each of the leaders in these examples would benefit from understanding the productive tension between measurable (quantitative) and visionary (qualitative) goals. As it stands, they've chosen structure over soul, or vice versa.

Unwanted results are usually symptoms of neglect. When something essential is ignored—whether meaning or measurement—the gap eventually shows up in outcomes you don't want.

Paradox-aware leaders don't pick. They balance, shift, and stretch between both.

Finding Your North Star: Qualitative Goals

After the layoff experience I described at the start of the chapter, I became more aware of what teams actually talk about when the metrics aren't on the screen. What usually gets people excited isn't hitting a number—it's solving a real customer problem. It's making something beautiful. It's knowing the work *means* something.

That's what qualitative goals do. They name the meaning. They give your team a reason to care, even when the charts aren't climbing. Author Simon Sinek calls it starting with your "why." Which is slightly harder than starting with coffee, but infinitely more energizing.

Think about Disney. The "why" that Walt seems to have believed is: "Create magical experiences." That simple vision has fueled decades of innovation. Same with the Dutch Bros Coffee company I mentioned earlier. Their mission is: "Fuel and uplift lives." Selling an OK drive-through brew could feel pedestrian, but to the degree that they live into their vision, it's not marketing fluff. It's an anchor.

Qualitative goals don't shift every quarter. They hold steady when the metrics wobble. They remind your team what game they're playing—and why it matters.

So here's the question: Does your team have a North Star? And if so—do they know they're allowed to steer by it?

Translating Purpose into Practice

A good mission statement feels like a compass. A great one feels like gravity—it pulls decisions, energy, and attention into alignment without shouting.

Disney's mission isn't just to entertain—it's to *enchant*. That's the difference between releasing a movie and creating a memory. During economic downturns, when budgets tighten and markets shift, that simple purpose—"Create magical experiences"—has been their tether. It's what kept teams innovating even when stockholders were bracing for impact.

Dutch Bros Coffee runs on a similar current. Their goal isn't just to sell coffee—it's to "Uplift lives." So when they invest in leadership training, or pay for someone's therapy, or send a barista to speak at a school assembly—it's not a bonus. It's the mission in action. That's what turns culture into momentum.

Even tech giants need this. Google's purpose—"Organize the world's information and make it universally accessible and useful"—isn't flashy. But it's remarkably sticky. It's why engineers obsessed over nano-second load times and UX teams redesigned interfaces with almost parental care. The clarity of purpose didn't make their measurable goals easier—it made them *inevitable*.

That's the pattern: When teams know why they're doing the work, the metrics get sharper. When they don't, even wins can feel flat.

So if your team's achievements feel technically impressive but emotionally muted—pause. The problem might not be effort. It might be orientation.

Tuning the Tension: Practical Tools

Tools don't fix things on their own. But the right ones, used with intention, can change everything.

Start with SMART goals: Specific. Measurable. Achievable. Relevant. Time-bound. You've probably seen this list a dozen times, maybe in an HR handbook gathering dust next to the fire escape plan. But used well, SMART goals are less about structure—and more about honesty. A fuzzy goal avoids accountability. A SMART goal says: *This is what matters, and this is when we'll know.*

Then there are the key performance indicators (KPIs). The key word isn't "performance." It's "key." A good KPI tells you something meaningful. A bad one tells you someone's trying too hard to look good on a slide deck for the board of directors. It's useful here to mention vanity metrics. These are numbers that look great in a presentation and tell you absolutely nothing. Think: total likes, click counts, or screenshots of an inbox with zero unaddressed emails. Pretty, but hollow. If a metric doesn't help you make a better decision, it's probably vanity.

This third tool is the one I believe to be the powerhouse: objectives and key results (OKRs). Think of them as a handshake between your soul and your spreadsheet. The objective is qualitative—bold, inspiring, clear. The key results are measurable—specific, focused, and few.

A good OKR sounds like this:

- **Objective**: Deliver an onboarding experience employees rave about.

- **Key Results**: Reduce onboarding time by 25 percent. Increase new hire satisfaction score to 90 percent. Complete peer mentorship rollout by the end of the third fiscal quarter.

That's what it looks like when purpose meets precision.

The first time I used OKRs was in the context of a strategic initiative to move beyond our primary market—a necessary step for the growth we desired. In a quarterly planning meeting we identified three essential metrics that would let us know if we were on the right track or not.

We missed our targets, as it turned out. And that was critical information. Without those clear and unfudgeable numbers to keep us honest, we would have done what we had often done before: Find something else both positive and irrelevant to call attention to, declare victory, and keep chugging down the same wrong track. The numbers forced us to change direction.

Mastering Measurable Goals

Qualitative goals give us purpose. But at some point, someone has to ask, "Are we actually getting anywhere?" That's where measurable goals come in. They bring clarity. They mark progress. They let you celebrate something more concrete than "Vibes are up."

But clarity without care can get weird fast.

I once led an engineering team with a couple of members who struggled with productivity. So I introduced a dangerous success metric: lines of code committed. It was dangerous because bad software code is bloated by unnecessary lines. Great code is lean, efficient, and easier to maintain. It also takes more time and thought. If that metric had been allowed to continue after it had served its specific purpose, it would have become a dangerous perverse incentive.

This is the leadership tension again: Measurable goals give you focus, but if you don't hold them in tension with meaning, they start shaping behavior in ways that miss the point. That's the shadow side of metrics: when we start measuring what's easy instead of what matters.

Great measurable goals aren't flashy. They're focused. They help your team answer:

- Are we better than we were?
- Are we moving in the right direction?
- Are we doing something that matters to someone?

And let's be honest—having too many goals is its own form of chaos. Three well-chosen metrics beat 15 mediocre measures every day of the week. Metrics overflow means what you're measuring isn't actually progress.

Team Exercise: Clarifying Your Why

It's easy to assume your team knows the "why" behind their work. After all, it's in the mission statement. It was in a slide deck sometime last year. And you've probably even said it out loud more than once.
But here's a better test:

1. In a team meeting or 1:1, ask: "Why does your work matter—to you?" Give space. Let them answer honestly. Not what sounds good. What feels real.
2. Ask the follow-up: "How does that connect to what we're trying to do as a team?" Listen for the bridges—where personal purpose and team purpose overlap.
3. Then ask: "What's a concrete way we'll know we're moving toward that?" That's your measurable anchor.

The intent of this exercise is to illuminate alignment, or the lack of it. When people name their own meaning, you don't have to motivate them. You just have to help them move.

Navigating the Moment of Neglect

You may have had times in your working life when your metrics look good, but it feels like something's gone missing. I've experienced times when "success," as indicated by most outward measures, didn't feel like success. It felt . . . hollow.

Maybe your qualitative vision feels mysterious, outdated, or mostly ignored. Or maybe you've been riding high on purpose, full of passion, but can't quite explain what progress actually looks like. Either way, you're feeling a quiet sense of drift.

This isn't failure. It's a checkpoint. It's the moment where awareness returns—and with it, the possibility of renewal. Paradox-aware leadership isn't about never losing sight of the balance. It's about noticing when one side is starved—and choosing to feed it again.

So if you're feeling that tension—good. That means you're paying attention. That's where paradox-aware leadership begins.

Overcoming Resistance and Facilitating Change

Inviting your team into productive tension won't always be welcome. Resistance to progress doesn't always show up as shouting. Sometimes, it's the quiet nod. The polite delay. The to-do item that keeps slipping to "next week."

You propose integrating qualitative and measurable goals—and someone on your team immediately says: "Sure. But . . . what does that actually mean?" You can choose, in that moment, to appreciate their vulnerability. The kind of change that asks people to think differently isn't just logical, it's emotional. People aren't resisting your idea. They're protecting what they already know how to do.

So meet the resistance with clarity, not control.

- Explain *why* you're shifting.
- Share what it unlocks, not just what it replaces.
- Invite people to help shape the change—not just comply with it.

Most of all, remember: You're not just adjusting a strategy. You're rewriting some of the mental models that have kept your team safe. Honor that. And walk with them.

Embracing Productive Tension

At any given time, you may feel more drawn to a need for either inspiration or clarity, to purpose or to precision. The natural impulse is to solve it. Pick one. Favor what feels most urgent.

But what if the tension *isn't* the problem? What if it's the signal that you're finally leading at the level that matters?

Productive tension means choosing to live in the stretch between story and structure, between meaning and measurement, between how it feels and how it's tracked.

Weak teams avoid this. They simplify. They flatten. They favor what's easiest to quantify. But great teams learn to breathe in the paradox. They let purpose drive action and let outcomes refine purpose.

You don't have to resolve the tension. You have to *relate to it differently.* Not as something to fix, but as something to *grow into.*

Reaping Clarity and Purpose

If you're feeling the tension between qualitative and measurable goals, you're in a good place. It means you're paying attention.

A polarized leader will either chase metrics without meaning or speak to broad purpose without proof. A paradox-aware leader stays long enough in the discomfort to see the shape of something better.

You now know:

- Metrics matter when they reflect real progress.
- Vision matters when you can measure progress.
- Tension isn't the enemy, it's the engine.

Whatever your initial inclinations, your efforts to honor both produce powerful clarity. You still measure. But you measure with purpose. You still cast vision. But you cast it with traction.

Paradox-aware leadership dignifies your work and makes you a steward of meaning. I've lived both sides—obsessed with metrics and intoxicated by vision. But the real breakthroughs happened when I started holding them together as coauthors of meaningful progress.

Key Takeaways

- **The numbers can say you're winning while your gut whispers you're drifting.** Measurable progress without meaning is motion without momentum.
- **Qualitative goals anchor your team in purpose.** They name what matters when no one's watching the dashboard.
- **Metrics don't need to be loud—they need to be honest.** Vanity metrics impress. Key metrics guide.
- **The tension is real: structure versus soul, progress versus purpose.** Great teams don't resolve this tension—they learn to lead inside it.
- **Purpose without measurement is poetry with no legs.** Measurement without purpose is math with no heart. You need both.
- **SMART goals and OKRs are clarifiers.** When used well, they bring transparency and traction to your team's priorities.
- **Organizational drift often begins with neglected vision or bloated metrics.** Regular check-ins with your "why" prevent those detours.
- **Paradox-aware leaders don't flatten the complexity.** They breathe in the tension and translate it into clarity, energy, and meaningful work.

CHAPTER 7

Flexibility Versus Grit

"Stay flexible."

"Adapt quickly."

These are do-or-die leadership maxims that have been drilled into me all my working life. Admittedly, I've spent my career in tech companies and startups. In that world, there is a whole category of team management methodologies known as "agile" development. Rapid change is doctrine if you're running a software as a service (SaaS) company. In that world, evolution isn't optional—it's survival. If you pause to catch your breath, someone faster is already shipping version 2.0 and eating your lunch. Tech companies value flexibility.

I know that other businesses and organizations don't run that way.

I consulted once with executives at a 125-year-old insurance company. We were sitting in a sunlit boardroom with polished wood furniture and a quietly ticking clock—a far cry from the whiteboards and folding desks I was used to. We were talking about the software project I was building for them when one of their executives leaned back and said that they were not a "projects company." I nodded politely, hoping that with a little time for reflection I'd figure out what a "projects company" was. Coming from a fast-moving tech background, it took me longer than I like to admit to wrap my head around it.

It turns out that "projects" are short-term initiatives. Projects are not what the insurance company was built for. Their operating maxims were more along the lines of "slow and steady" and "stay the course."

Their business and reputation was built on reliable actuarial tables and averages observed across time. Changes and adjustments had to be minor and always preceded by volumes of data. They were built to outlast any passing storm. They valued grit.

Beyond business model differences, I've observed that the style of individual leaders often leans either to flexibility or grit. Some go easily with the flow and others resist a running stream. Perhaps you recognize a preference within yourself. Maybe you live for the thrill of rapid iteration. Or maybe your strength is slow-burning persistence.

Whichever your preference and whatever your business, you will at some point feel this tension personally. The world is changing fast enough that even insurance executives have to adapt. And as technology companies age, their leaders must articulate an enduring center to survive.

Welcome to the productive tension between flexibility and grit.

Navigating the Storm

Let's say your organization is faced with a sudden, dramatic change. Maybe it's a market disruption, like a new technology that makes part of what you do obsolete almost overnight. Perhaps it's a crisis that arrives without warning, like a global pandemic transforming work in a matter of weeks. In these moments, your instincts might shout conflicting advice. One voice says, *Hold steady, be persistent, stay the course!* Another equally credible voice warns, *Pivot now! Adapt or perish!*

In 2008, Howard Schultz sensed that Starbucks had lost its soul. The stores felt cluttered and rushed more than welcoming and inviting. The smell of warm pastries was weaker than that of plastic and burnt beans. So Schultz did something unthinkable: He closed 7,100 US stores for a day of culture retraining. Investors panicked. Headlines mocked him. But Schultz was playing a longer game—recentering the company not just on coffee, but on connection. That's flexibility. It's the courage to pivot—to admit something isn't working, and change it before it's too late.

James Dyson is a model of the opposite virtue. Before launching his first vacuum, he spent five years creating 5,127 prototypes. He wasn't chasing trends. He was doggedly pursuing precision. Grit is that kind of stubborn. It keeps after a single goal when others would have pivoted away. It believes in the problem long enough to earn the breakthrough.

These are both leadership virtues, but they rarely live in harmony. That's the storm. There is value in both reinvention and a refusal to bend. Paradox-aware leaders learn to ride out the storm in a way that honors both.

Finding Your Guide

Flexibility is crucial. Research into modern leadership emphasizes how adaptive leaders excel in dynamic environments, swiftly changing tactics as conditions evolve. Leaders who embrace flexibility enable innovation and resilience, adapting their methods while preserving their core mission. Take Reed Hastings, former CEO of Netflix. His willingness to risk everything that once defined Netflix by pivoting from DVD rentals to streaming demonstrates how flexibility in action can secure future success.

Yet, grit—the relentless pursuit of long-term goals despite setbacks—remains equally essential. Angela Duckworth's extensive research, encapsulated in her groundbreaking book *Grit*, highlights persistence as a critical predictor of long-term success. One of Duckworth's favorite examples is Jeff Bezos, the founder of Amazon. Bezos was relentless in his vision for building the most customer-centric company in the world. He made long-term investments in warehouses and data centers to provide wider selection and faster delivery, even though many critics told him he should focus on near-term profitability instead.

As a leader, you now have two guiding lights: flexibility and grit. But how can you follow both simultaneously without losing your way?

Expecting Mistakes

Here's the uncomfortable truth about paradox-aware leadership: At some point, you're going to fail in balancing these competing virtues. Perhaps you'll persevere too long on a failing initiative, confusing stubbornness for grit. Or maybe you'll pivot too quickly, abandoning promising ideas at the first sign of difficulty. Each misstep, though painful, teaches invaluable lessons.

Take Airbnb, for example. In early 2020, they were riding high—luxury travel, business rentals, global expansion. The roadmap was bold, the vision inspiring.

Then COVID-19 hit. Travel collapsed. Bookings vanished. Suddenly, their big plans looked not just off-track, but tone-deaf.

CEO Brian Chesky didn't have a clean playbook for a crisis like this. Some early decisions misfired. Messaging was inconsistent. A few experiments fell flat. And yet, through the chaos, a pattern began to emerge.

Chesky paused expansion projects. He made painful layoffs—but did it with rare transparency and care. He shifted focus to long-term stays, rural listings, and the core emotional thread that had built the company to begin with: belonging.

It wasn't neat. It wasn't flawless. But it was honest.

Airbnb didn't push through by sheer force, and they didn't abandon their identity. They flexed. They stumbled. They recalibrated. And because they stayed grounded in their purpose, they came through stronger—not in spite of the mess, but *because* they were willing to move through it.

That's what paradox-aware leadership looks like in the tension between flexibility and grit: holding direction and adaptation at the same time—especially when the path forward is anything but clear.

I've had my own moments of hanging on too long. We once poured years into a product that prospects said they wanted, but in the end, would seldom buy. It was painful for me to let go of something that had been largely my idea to begin with. It wasn't until a long look at our cost of acquiring a customer (CAC) numbers that I was forced to see how I was mistaking grit for stubbornness.

Paradox-aware leaders expect to make mistakes as they find a way to honor both grit and flexibility. By embracing the value of each, they strive to recognize errors early, learn deeply, and continuously recalibrate their balance.

Effective Examples

The growth ordeal emerges not from choosing flexibility over grit, or vice versa, but from understanding their interplay. Flexibility without grit leads to fickleness; grit without flexibility leads to rigidity. Paradox-aware leaders hold both in productive tension. I realize this can sound like an impossibly tall order. A couple of examples of success may be helpful at this point.

In 2006, Ford was in freefall—losing billions, bleeding morale, and headed for the kind of government bailout that would later define the Great Recession. Along came Alan Mulally.

He didn't arrive with bombast. He was committed to a single long-term idea: *One Ford*—a simple, unifying vision to replace decades of siloed divisions and turf wars. It was bold. It was clean. And he refused to compromise on it.

But grit alone wasn't enough. As market conditions shifted and financial panic set in, Mulally adjusted course—slashing waste, retooling operations, rethinking supply chains. He held the line on the long-term vision, but flexed almost everything else.

When the dust settled, Ford was the only major US automaker that hadn't taken a government bailout.

That's paradox-aware leadership in the wild: a vision that doesn't blink, and a strategy that never stays still.

One more example: Sending anything to Mars is not simple. But the NASA project called *Perseverance* lived up to its name before it even left the launch pad.

Engineers faced delay after delay—weather, mechanical issues, launch complications. Still, they pushed forward, holding tight to an audacious mission: Land a new rover, fly a helicopter in Martian air, and search for signs of ancient life.

But what made the mission succeed wasn't just technical grit—it was *adaptive* brilliance. Mid-mission, teams rewrote flight plans, updated rover software from 140 million miles away, and rerouted the rover to unexpected terrain.

For me, as a software builder and a problem solver, the sheer chutzpah required to rewrite software from 140 million miles away hits close to home. It reminds me that adaptation doesn't mean abandoning purpose—it means rewriting the rules in real time.

The success was philosophical as well as scientific. The *Perseverance* team persisted and they evolved. Grit met flexibility and history was made.

Personal Application

As you develop your own paradox-awareness, you'll see that flexibility and grit aren't enemies but allies—each incomplete without the other.

In the process of application you'll realize that balance requires continuously adjusting tension between competing values.

This understanding transforms your approach to everyday challenges. You won't reactively swing like a pendulum from one extreme to the other. You become capable of nuanced judgment, feeling out in time- and place-specific ways when to stand firm and when to adjust course.

In the process of application you'll realize that balance requires continuously adjusting tension between competing values. The interplay between grit and flexibility becomes your greatest strength, enabling innovation, resilience, and sustained progress.

Newfound Power

Appreciation of this particular paradox gives you a powerful new perspective. You now appreciate that flexibility is strategic adaptability and balanced grit is courageous perseverance informed by reality. On teams that you lead to honor this tension, trust will deepen, morale will improve, and innovation will blossom as everyone begins to embrace the productive tension you've cultivated.

Paradox-awareness gives you confidence that there is always a way to navigate through the apparent contradiction. You have to believe in the way paradoxes work to be willing to search for that way. By giving both flexibility and grit equal respect, you set your team up for sustainable, transformative success.

As I've worked on my own paradox-aware leadership, the journey itself has been my greatest teacher. I've decided that SaaS startups and insurance companies share a common need to tune their focus to the demands of their circumstances. I can learn to do that. So can you.

When you feel caught between opposing truths, the tension isn't something to eliminate, it's something to harness. It's a superpower—and now it's yours.

Key Takeaways

- **Flexibility and grit are both essential leadership virtues.** Great leaders know how to flex without flailing, and persevere without calcifying.
- **Your instincts will often contradict each other.** That's a signal you're in a paradox worth exploring.
- **Paradox-aware leaders expect to get it wrong sometimes.** That's part of the process. Mistakes become data. The goal is recalibration, not perfection.
- **Flexibility without grit leads to volatility. Grit without flexibility leads to rigidity.** Either extreme can break you. Held in tension, they make you unbreakable.
- **Holding paradox is a practice, not a finish line.** It requires presence, emotional maturity, and clarity of purpose—qualities that grow with each challenge.
- **You don't have to choose between bending and holding firm.** You have to learn how to do both—well, and at the right time.

CHAPTER 8

Cocreation Versus Directional Clarity

When Satya Nadella took the reins at Microsoft in 2014, he inherited a company at war with itself. Silos had stifled collaboration. Innovation had stalled. The once-dominant tech giant felt slow and tired.

I remember watching Nadella's early interviews and being struck by how much humility he brought to a company known for sharp elbows. His shift in tone alone felt revolutionary.

Nadella faced a classic leadership paradox: Should he painstakingly cocreate a vision with thousands of employees—risking an avalanche of PowerPoints and a thousand shades of "meh"—or boldly declare a new path, bracing for the inevitable flood of politely barbed feedback?

What would you do?

Embracing the Tension

It's easy to find examples that seem to argue for the primacy of either cocreation or directional clarity.

In 2006, IBM tapped its own latent internal genius by committing $100 million to a crowdsourcing exercise called "Innovation Jam." Over 150,000 employees participated, ultimately launching 10 new businesses that no top-down strategy could have unearthed.

By contrast, Ford began its revival that same year, powered by Alan Mulally's unifying mantra: *One Ford*. No committee. No ambiguity. Just clarity, fiercely held.

So at first glance, cocreation and directional clarity seem like leadership opposites. Cocreation invites ownership and surfaces hidden wisdom. Directional clarity provides unity and momentum.

In my own experience leading cross-functional teams, I've seen how alignment and inclusion can feel at odds—especially when deadlines loom. In reality, it's not which pole you favor, it's how you hold the tension between them that defines your leadership. If you treat them like an either/or binary, something breaks.

Recognizing the Moment

Most leaders will, at some point, face a crossroads where new direction is needed. In that moment, you might pull your team together for a series of co-creative workshops. The risk in this approach is weeks of sticky notes, strained patience, and a direction that still feels uncertain at the end of it.

Alternatively, you could stand at the whiteboard and just say, "Here's where we're going." Bad outcomes from this approach include eye rolls, passivity, silent resistance, or even disengagement.

At LEGO, they faced this paradox head-on in the early 2000s. Sales were slipping and their brand was fading. In response, they launched "LEGO Ideas," inviting fans to cocreate future sets. Simultaneously, senior leaders laid down a clear strategy: Become the most innovative, consumer-driven toy company in the world.

They didn't toggle between collaboration and command. They did both.

The Courage to Cocreate

Cocreation sounds inspiring—like a friendly brainstorming session with snacks. But the kind that shapes a team's future is not for the faint of heart.

Why? Because true cocreation requires courage. It asks leaders to surrender control, to open up decisions to perspectives that may challenge their assumptions or even their identity. It involves the very real possibility that your idea might not be the right one, even if you've spent sleepless nights nurturing it. You have to start with the belief that someone else's idea might be better.

It also carries emotional risk. When leaders invite others into the creative process, they risk discomfort, slowdowns, disagreement, and ambiguity. They risk losing perceived authority. They risk vulnerability. Cocreation is not consensus-seeking or decision-by-committee. It's something more profound: a deliberate act of shared ownership that honors collective wisdom without dissolving clarity.

But the payoff is immense. When people feel ownership over an idea, their engagement skyrockets. They work not just harder but smarter. They challenge ideas early—when it still helps—and commit fully once the direction is set. And perhaps most importantly, they become co-stewards of the outcomes, not just passive executors of someone else's plan.

I've spent a lot of time in Fresno, California. Central California is a hot and dry farming region—a world away from the greenery and glamor of coastal California. I was intrigued to hear this story about the Fresno Unified School District in California, one of the largest in the state. In the early 2000s, the district faced declining performance, high dropout rates, and serious trust deficits between administrators and teachers. A new superintendent, Michael Hanson, took a bold approach—not by issuing top-down mandates, but by cocreating a vision with teachers, parents, students, and community leaders.

Early meetings were tense. Teachers voiced frustrations, and many expected another round of empty promises. But the leadership persisted, holding listening sessions, gathering data, and—crucially—adjusting plans in response to what they heard. One key move was codeveloping new instructional frameworks with teacher-led design teams. The process was messy. There were walkouts. There were rewrites. But ultimately, what emerged was a system of shared accountability and improvement that the whole community owned.

Over time, Fresno Unified's graduation rates rose dramatically, and teacher retention improved. The district's courageous cocreation didn't just improve test scores—it restored trust.

That's what makes cocreation brave. Not that it's soft or slow or people-pleasing, but that it requires leaders to bet on their people. It asks them to trust that the best path forward may emerge not from their brilliance alone, but from the space they create for others to contribute.

The Clarity of Bold Vision

If cocreation demands courage, so does its counterpart: the bold articulation of vision. Naming a direction—clearly and without apology—always entails risk. You risk being wrong. You risk not being followed. You risk committing to a future that others may not yet see. But clarity, when it comes from a place of deep alignment and integrity, can be one of the greatest gifts a leader offers.

A clear vision is compelling not because it dictates every step of the journey, but because it dares to paint a future worth striving for. The best visions connect to something shared—values already alive in the hearts of others, even if unnamed. They lift people out of the transactional and into the transformational. They help us feel that *this is where we're going, and I want to be part of it.*

Vision becomes magnetic when it's both bold and believable—when it stretches our imagination but still feels within reach. It doesn't need to be a grand speech. Sometimes, it's a single sentence that reframes everything: "A computer on every desk." "Every child reading by third grade." "A place where no one is invisible." The most powerful visions are lived stories waiting to be told, not abstract slogans laminated on the wall.

And perhaps most importantly, a compelling vision gives everyone a role. It doesn't describe a leader's solo plan—it invites others to join as coauthors of the story. People follow when they see themselves in the picture. They commit when the path ahead is infused with purpose, not just instruction.

That's why vision is not just a matter of communication. It's an act of leadership. An act of faith. It says, "I believe this is possible. I believe it's worth it. And I believe we can do it together."

When President John F. Kennedy declared in 1961 that the United States would put a man on the moon and return him safely to Earth before the decade was out, he wasn't responding to a committee consensus. He was naming a direction few thought possible. The technology didn't yet exist. The path was uncertain. The risks—technological, political, even moral—were enormous. But Kennedy provided clarity of purpose summed up in one sentence that turned a daunting technical ambition into a shared challenge: "Not because it is easy," he said in a speech at Rice University, "but because it is hard." Millions were inspired, and supported the effort because they wanted to be part of something worthy of the risk.

A few years later, Dr. Martin Luther King Jr. stood on the steps of the Lincoln Memorial and described a world that did not yet exist—a world where children would be judged by the content of their character rather than the color of their skin. His clarity, too, was dangerous. He faced resistance, arrests, even death threats. But the vision he cast was morally anchored and widely resonant. He gave people a way to imagine justice not as an abstract principle but as a real and reachable horizon. His words clarified not just what the civil rights movement was fighting against but what it was fighting for.

In both cases, bold vision acted as a compass. It didn't eliminate risk. It didn't offer certainty. But it united people around a shared purpose. And that clarity became the seed of extraordinary progress.

The Danger of Overcorrection

If you feel like your team is lacking either buy-in or clear direction, there is another risk, you should consider: overcorrection.

In Yahoo's early 2000s decline, leadership cycled through vision after vision—bold new directions launched from the top, often with minimal buy-in or ground-level insight. Strategy shifted faster than teams could keep up. Morale frayed, execution stalled, and Yahoo slowly faded from the center of the internet it had once helped define. I've worked in organizations where we swerved from strategy to strategy without taking the time to learn from what didn't work. It's exhausting—and avoidable.

On the flip side, consider Mozilla in the post-Firefox boom. Known for its democratic, consensus-driven culture, Mozilla often struggled to ship major innovations. Multiple promising browser ideas floundered—not because they lacked talent but because no one could drive the final decision forward.

Vision without collaboration fractures trust. Collaboration without clarity stalls momentum. Either alone is risky. The power is in the paradox.

Navigating the Productive Tension

To lead effectively, you must navigate between these poles, dynamically adjusting your approach to preserve a productive tension. Consider again the NASA Mars Rover *Perseverance* mission as an exceptional illustration of navigating this tension. NASA provided crystal-clear mission objectives paired with detailed measurable goals. United by this clear directive, the NASA teams employed deep cocreation across engineering, scientific communities, and global partners. The combination of clear direction and cocreation delivered unprecedented innovation, overcoming challenges no single group could have managed alone.

Had NASA relied only on hierarchy, *Perseverance* never would've flown. Had they relied only on consensus, they'd still be debating landing zones.

Transformative Leadership Emerges

Mastering this paradox leads to transformative outcomes. Leaders capable of honoring both cocreation and directional clarity craft resilient, innovative organizations that thrive in complexity. Under Nadella, Microsoft didn't just pivot—it performed the strategic equivalent of a triple backflip, sticking the landing so gracefully that even the Russian judges were impressed. Nadella provided directional clarity with a unifying vision: empowering individuals and organizations through technology. He also fostered a culture of profound collaboration and empathy. Teams actively participated in shaping strategies that were unified by a clear, inspiring purpose. What emerged was a revitalized organizational culture, market-leading innovation, and sustained growth.

Nadella didn't toggle between cocreation and command. He fused them. His example highlights something interesting about how paradox-aware leadership works. When a leader honors two competing goods—both sides of a paradox—a harmony emerges that's better than either good on its own could produce. Unified and harmonized teams are like orchestras—they make music no single instrument, or person, could create alone.

By choosing not to choose between competing goods, paradox-aware leaders orchestrate them into something even better.

Key Takeaways

- **Cocreation and clarity are complementary strengths.** When held together, they create momentum without mutiny and alignment without alienation.

- **Over-indexing on clarity risks disengagement. Over-indexing on collaboration risks inertia.** You can't whiteboard your way out of ambiguity, nor can you command your way into innovation.

- **Cocreation builds trust and surfaces wisdom.** Directional clarity galvanizes energy and cuts through fog. Leaders must learn when to listen and when to lead.

- **You won't get it perfect—and that's the point.** Paradox-aware leadership isn't about always getting the tension right. It's about staying present enough to adjust, mid-stride, without losing heart or momentum.

- **The future won't be led by consensus or command alone.** It will be shaped by leaders who can harness the tension between them so that something better can emerge.

CHAPTER 9

Incremental Versus Impossible Goals

Y ou've probably heard both pieces of advice: Set small, achievable goals; and set goals so big they scare you.

Maybe, like me, you've tried both—whiplashing between extremes. One month, you have goals your grandmother could hit in her sleep. The next, they're so massive your therapist gently suggests "scaling back." One quarter not too long ago I felt so burned by spectacular failures in the quarter before that I thoughtfully set only goals I'd achieved before the quarter started—hoping no one else would notice. That went over poorly. So most of the time we mere mortal leaders manage the paradox by splitting the difference, setting goals big enough to brag about on LinkedIn, but small enough to abandon quietly by March.

When you aim small and steady, it feels responsible, but uninspiring. When you aim big, you end up overwhelmed or quietly ashamed when life pulls you off track. It can feel like you're stuck choosing between mediocrity and burnout.

The False Choice

In leadership, your goal-setting decisions impact everyone on your team, increasing the pressure to find an approach that works. But here, as in so many aspects of leadership, the script keeps flipping. One approach seems wise until the moment it doesn't. And every time you settle into a method, reality throws you a contradiction. That's where this chapter begins.

Maybe the tension you've felt isn't actually a mistake or a contradiction. Maybe it's precisely the thing that makes the difference. It might seem like a contradiction—until you see what it really looks like to *live* inside the paradox.

Seeing the Paradox Clearly

What if the tension between incremental and impossible goals isn't something to resolve, but something to embrace?

As with other paradoxes, I argue that there is power—massive, catalytic power—in holding both ideas at once. In seeing that impossible-feeling goals give us high purpose, and incremental goals give us measurable progress. That's the productive crux of the tension. And it's a place you can lead from.

It would be fair if you argued that this sounds good in theory, but it is hard to implement. People who go all-in on impossible goals talk about moonshots, vision, audacity. They get the glory. People who swear by atomic habits talk about systems, structure, and compound interest. They get the results.

So why would you risk mixing them? Isn't that just indecision dressed up in spin?

It might seem that way. Until you see what it really looks like to live inside the paradox.

Two Powerful Schools of Thought

Let's look closely at the argument for each side.

First, James Clear and the "atomic habits" school of thought. Clear's premise in his book *Atomic Habits* is that small changes, made consistently, create profound transformation. He cites Sir Dave Brailsford and the British cycling team as an example of how 1 percent improvements in hundreds of tiny areas—the aggregation of marginal gains—led to a stunning reversal of a century of mediocrity. Not through heroics, but through margin.

Then there's Dan Sullivan and Ben Hardy with their book *10x is easier than 2x*. They argue that truly great progress never comes from small changes. It requires a new identity, a new game. They offer the Renaissance man Michelangelo as evidence. He literally broke the law and risked his life to dissect cadavers to understand human anatomy and thereby sculpt more accurately. That's not something you do for the sake of a 1 percent improvement. That's the kind of risk you take when you desperately want an impossible goal. He wanted stone figures so lifelike they might almost inhale and walk off their base. This level of skill shift requires a total self-reinvention.

To strengthen the argument for the 10x school, I would add the simple observation that Sir David Brailsford wasn't driven by a vision of incremental gains for their own sake. He was intensely demanding about these minor changes because his goal was impossibly high. He wanted olympic gold and the yellow jersey of the Tour de France.

In support of atomic habits, I argue that, along with his impossible goal, Michelangelo also had a thousand minor goals and work habits that took him there. To learn and to see what lay beneath the human skin, he made a plan that began with finding out when and where the very poor of Florence were buried. He then discretely negotiated an exchange with the prior of the Santo Spirito church, trading a carved wooden crucifix for access to rooms where he could perform the dissections. He habituated himself to a nightly discipline of anatomical study, incrementally deepening his knowledge week by week. He did this for years. He didn't just take a single reckless leap. He established disciplined, incremental habits. He studied by candlelight, methodically cultivated alliances, and practiced relentlessly. Each of these habits systematically built his capacity to achieve the impossible.

Atomic thinkers say, "Habits make identity," whereas 10x thinkers say, "Identity *demands* new habits." The paradox-aware leader says, "Both are true—if you want your goal to change you."

Here's what it might look like for you to begin navigating this paradox.

Paradox in Practice

Perhaps you imagine a version of yourself who is leaner, more focused, more alive. Not just 10 pounds lighter, but living in a body and rhythm that feels deeply right. You see that future self vividly. That's your 10x goal.

Then you ask yourself: *What needs to be true to become that person?* You build routines. Change your environment. Eliminate the noise. You begin making 1 percent changes that align with your goal. You aren't hustling. You're methodically becoming.

You build the routines. You stock the fridge. You get eight hours of sleep and buy a water bottle with motivational time stamps.

And then . . . resistance shows up.

The spouse who tells you to "just be realistic." The colleague who rolls their eyes at your big vision. The internal voice that says, *Who do you think you are?*

You also find allies. A friend who holds you accountable. A mentor who shares their own impossible goal. A team member who catches your vision.

You learn that paradox-aware leadership isn't solo heroism. It's courage with support. It's creating a space where the pursuit of the impossible feels rational and grounded.

This is what I experienced when I walked away from a company I helped found and had loved for more than a decade. I did it because I could see a version of myself that would only come to be when I accepted the risks and rewards of a brand new venture.

You Will Hit the Wall

You should expect some days that break you down. You'll set a 10x goal, you'll commit, and it will fall apart.

Maybe your team doesn't buy in. Maybe the results don't come when you expect them. Maybe you hit a wall so hard it knocks the breath out of your confidence.

This is where leaders either retreat or transform. You realize the point of the goal wasn't the immediate outcome. It was what it demanded of you. What it forged in you. What you became in the pursuit.

Michelangelo became a different artist—not because of the outcome (what he sculpted) but because of what he learned when he took the risks necessary to sculpt. You become a different leader—not because you achieve success with any specific goal but because the discomfort of the process demands that you become something greater than what you were.

You aren't defined by the heroic summit—but by the storm that makes you question the climb and the choice you make in that moment.

Who You Become

An impossible goal gives you focus, because while there may be hundreds of ways to achieve a modest goal, very few paths are viable to reach a goal that feels impossible. There are many flights, trains, and roads that will get you to Kathmandu, the capital of Nepal. But only a few dangerous routes actually lead to Everest's summit. Once you know your impossible goal, your incremental goals are the essential steps that simplify the task at hand. Those daily milestones let you cut through the overwhelm and the noise. They give you each successive anchor point, foothold, and safe belay necessary for your ascent.

I've never climbed Everest, but I know what it's like to stand before a goal so steep I wasn't sure which step came next. Impossible goals focus your vision. Incremental goals focus your steps.

One gives you Everest. The other gives you the map.

When your team starts to trust the process, it won't be because you have all the answers but because you've modeled iteration, courage, and curiosity. There has been a point in each company I've led where I realized the goal wasn't just a better product. It was becoming someone who could lead a team through ambiguity.

Leading from Tension

When you are a leader who is aware of the paradox between incremental and impossible goals, you're not measuring success in outcomes alone, though those are essential. You're watching who you're becoming—and helping others become too.

You become someone who sees the world with new eyes.

You no longer seek safety in one school of thought. You lead from the tension.

You use 10x vision to ignite your imagination and atomic habits to build the road there.

This paradox-aware mindset gives you something rare:

Paradox-aware leadership is the art of walking into contradiction with clarity, not compromise.

A leadership identity that grows in tension, not despite it. A mental framework that holds ambition and humility, vision and discipline, impossible dreams and incremental progress—all at once. Paradox-aware leadership is the art of walking into contradiction with clarity, not compromise. It's holding a bold vision in one hand and a stopwatch in the other.

Paradox-awareness doesn't dilute your focus—it distills it. Impossible goals clarify direction; incremental goals clarify your daily decisions.

This is what your team needs. This is what your future self needs. This is what the world needs from you.

Key Takeaways

- **You don't have to choose between tiny goals and towering dreams.** Paradox-aware leadership invites you to hold both—impossible ambition and incremental progress.
- **Atomic habits and 10x thinking are not enemies.** One builds your structure. The other fuels your fire. The tension between them is where transformation lives.
- **Impossible goals forge identity.** They force you to become someone new—not by hoping, but by committing.
- **Incremental goals fuel progress.** They make big change digestible, visible, and sustainable. They give you a map for the climb.
- **You will face resistance—externally and internally.** Vision scares people. Change disrupts systems. Your doubt isn't proof you're wrong—it's part of the paradox.
- **Paradox-aware leaders integrate methods.** They light the torch of vision and then build the steps in darkness, one footfall at a time.

CHAPTER 10

Empathy Versus Accountability

Imagine this: Your top salesperson, we'll call her Emily, is usually a machine when it comes to quotas. Lately she has been slipping. Missed deadlines. Sloppy work. You know she's experiencing some serious strains in her personal life. Your heart goes out to her. But as the weeks go by, team members are noticing and wondering why she seems to get a perpetual pass. Whispers of favoritism are starting to swirl.

I've watched a high-performing team member falter during a personal crisis. My instinct was to shield them. But I've also seen how long delays in addressing performance can quietly erode team morale.

You want to be kind. You need to be fair. What do you do?

If you're like most leaders, your initial instinct might pull you sharply in one direction or the other. But paradox-aware leaders understand that true leadership excellence rarely comes from picking one side. Instead, it emerges from fully embracing the productive tension between two seemingly opposite virtues—in this case, empathy and accountability.

The Power of Empathy

Empathy is foundational to effective leadership. As leadership researcher Brené Brown highlights, empathy means understanding and connecting with your employees' emotions and experiences. It's about showing genuine care for their well-being, recognizing their humanity, and building deep trust. Companies such as Google, Patagonia, and Marriott have made empathy central to their leadership cultures, resulting in greater employee satisfaction, innovation, and even bottom-line results.

When Airbnb faced massive layoffs due to the COVID-19 pandemic, CEO Brian Chesky's empathetic approach made headlines. He didn't just send out a cold memo; he personally communicated with employees, expressed deep sorrow, and offered robust severance packages. The response from the public and employees alike reinforced how much empathy can strengthen an organization's culture and reputation during tough times.

But empathy can also become problematic if misapplied. Leaders who lean too far into empathy may find themselves tolerating consistent underperformance or avoiding difficult conversations, creating resentment among team members who must pick up the slack. Too much empathy with no accountability? It's like letting your kids have ice cream for dinner every night. Fun for a while—until someone gets a stomachache and nobody wants to eat broccoli ever again. Let's just say I've learned (the hard way) that trying to be everyone's favorite boss is a shortcut to being no one's trusted leader.

The Necessity of Accountability

On the other hand, accountability ensures clarity, fairness, and performance. Accountability-focused leaders set clear expectations, hold themselves and others answerable for results, and promptly address problems. The New York City Fire Department (FDNY) maintains one of the highest accountability standards in any public safety organization—without sacrificing humanity. Every firehouse operates on clear performance protocols, readiness checks, and after-action reviews.

Yet accountability has its pitfalls. When polarized, it can slide into blame, fear, and punishment. Push accountability too far, and your workplace starts feeling like a reality TV show: high drama, secret alliances, last-minute twists, and people praying not to get "voted off" in the next performance review. In 2016, Wells Fargo had a system of polarized accountability to aggressive sales targets that created a toxic, fear-driven culture, ultimately leading to widespread ethical breaches.

Leaders who stress accountability at the expense of empathy risk fostering environments where employees hide mistakes, resist taking risks, and disengage.

Navigating the Tension

Here's where paradox-aware leadership shines. Balancing empathy and accountability isn't about alternating between soft-heartedness and tough-mindedness. It's about recognizing that both virtues are essential, continuously pulling each other toward equilibrium. Leaders who navigate this tension skillfully create environments where accountability feels supportive rather than punitive, and empathy fuels high performance rather than excuses for falling short.

Earlier in my leadership journey, I thought I had to choose—be the nice guy or the enforcer. Paradox-awareness gave me a third option: Be clear and kind.

So let's return to Emily. Picture the hallway conversation outside the conference room. No scripts. No spreadsheets. Just you, her, and a tension that could tilt either way. What might a paradox-aware approach look like?

Empathy leads you to express genuine concern and listen. Acknowledge her struggles without immediately jumping to solutions. Empathy creates something called psychological safety—a shared belief held by members of a team that the team is safe for interpersonal risk-taking. Harvard researcher Amy Edmondson, one of the pioneers of research in the concept, argues that psychological safety allows for transparency and honest dialogue.

On that foundation, it's possible to speak honestly about expectations and responsibilities. Based on an understanding of her difficulties, it's possible to counsel together on the standards required for her role. Instead of lowering those standards, you can seek her input on how to offer practical support. Ideas might include temporarily redistributing tasks, a leave of absence, flexible deadlines, counseling, or coaching. This approach communicates accountability clearly but without harsh judgment.

Real-World Examples of Balance

I first became aware of the New Zealand All Blacks through friends who played on the rugby team at Brigham Young University (BYU). The All Blacks are one of the world's most successful sports teams. In his bestselling book *Legacy*, James Kerr describes a set of mantras that embody the culture of the team. One of them, "Embrace expectations," clearly emphasizes accountability. Others, like "Pass the ball" and "No dickheads," clearly emphasize empathetic concern for teammates ahead of personal achievement. Each team member is held strictly accountable for their behavior and performance. They're empowered to support one another, but never excused from their shared commitment to excellence.

I referenced earlier the structure and accountability protocols of the FDNY. Within those structures, there is a deep culture of brotherhood, peer mentoring, and emotional support, especially after high-trauma incidents. Leadership demands performance under pressure but recognizes a human toll. The result is an enduring culture where mutual accountability is paired with psychological support—firefighters hold each other to high standards because they care deeply for one another.

Finding Your Own Balance

Every leader will navigate the empathy-accountability tension differently. Your task isn't to replicate someone else's solution precisely, but to understand the paradox at play and consciously manage it with your own team.

If you struggle with this, as I have, you can ask yourself regularly: *Am I avoiding accountability because I fear conflict, or am I withholding empathy because I fear lowered standards?* Reflect honestly. Then course-correct.

The Transformative Journey

For me, this paradox is deeply personal. I've seen how clarity without compassion leads to burnout—and how compassion without clarity quietly poisons trust.

Mastering this tension is transformative. Over time, leaders who balance empathy and accountability shape healthier, more resilient teams. They create workplaces where everyone feels valued but also understands that performance matters. They inspire both loyalty and discipline. In short, they create cultures where both empathy and accountability can thrive.

Our hypothetical Emily can see what's expected, feel supported, and rise to the occasion. Maybe she takes some extended personal time to recalibrate and refocus. And the rest of the team will see fairness and leadership that holds space without lowering standards.

Cultivating the Paradox-Aware Mindset

As paradox-aware leaders, our ultimate goal isn't to "resolve" tension permanently. Rather, it's to maintain a steady, dynamic tension—like a string on a guitar tuned just right, vibrating clearly because it's held taut between two fixed points. This tension creates music in our leadership, fostering harmony and strength within our teams.

This is how paradox-aware leaders change the game, by tuning themselves to the music of leadership. Humanity *and* excellence. Care *and* clarity.

What these tensions all have in common is the way they trap us in frustration when left unnamed. Stuckness is not random—it is almost always the mark of a paradox in play. And paradox-awareness is what turns frustration into forward movement.

Key Takeaways

- **Empathy and accountability are twin pillars of sustainable leadership.** One fosters trust, the other ensures progress.
- **Empathy builds psychological safety.** It tells your team: "I see you, I value you." But empathy without accountability breeds resentment and low standards.
- **Accountability drives clarity and results.** It communicates: "We have goals, and they matter." But accountability without empathy creates fear and disengagement.

- **Paradox-aware leaders integrate both.** They create cultures where high expectations are paired with deep humanity.
- **You'll feel the tension.** And that's okay. It means you're paying attention. The goal is not comfort—it's courageous balance.
- **Great leadership feels like tuning an instrument.** You don't cut the strings to reduce tension—you learn how to make it sing.

Part 3

The Practice of Paradox-Aware Leadership

CHAPTER 11

Naming Your Paradoxes

This chapter will help you recognize the paradoxes actively at play in your own life and daily work. You'll learn practical tools to help you clearly identify and name these tensions. By applying these straightforward yet powerful strategies, you'll learn to bring your paradoxes into the light—transforming confusion into clarity and paralysis into meaningful progress.

Important Note: Meaningful progress assumes that you know what your goals are and that your team is aligned as described in Chapter 5. Knowing what your goals are means having both a compass point and measurable milestones as you saw in Chapter 6. Chapter 14 will give you more tools for team alignment.

A Practical Process for Naming Paradoxes

This practical process is adapted from Kegan and Lahey's Immunity to Change model, which provides structured guidance for tracing emotions and behaviors back to hidden beliefs and competing commitments.

1. Start with Emotions

Begin by recognizing when you feel emotionally stuck, confused, anxious, or frustrated. Look for red flags such as ongoing stress, avoidance of certain tasks or conversations, procrastination, defensive reactions to criticism, or a persistent sense of feeling blocked or ineffective. These strong, unclear emotions often signal a paradox or hidden tension.

2. Identify Counterproductive Behaviors

Following the trail of those emotions, look for unproductive patterns or issues that repeatedly surface in your interactions or outcomes. One of the most useful concepts taught by James Clear is that our life choices, habits, and patterns optimize us for the results we are getting. If you are in any way unhappy with your results, you have the power to choose different patterns.

Focus attention on your own role within these patterns. Are there specific behaviors or decisions you make—or avoid making—that seem to maintain or worsen your confusion or discomfort? Also look for signals from others. Do your colleagues ever express concerns about your collaboration patterns in communication or teamwork?

The temptation will be for you to attribute difficulties solely to external factors—your team, your boss, the universe, etc. Remember, though, that the goal is to uncover your own counterproductive patterns. This takes courage. It's usually helpful to enlist a coach or trusted friend to help with this. A good friend will be invested enough in your progress to share unvarnished truth as they see it.

3. Reveal Hidden Competing Commitments

When you identify a counterproductive pattern—something you are doing that seems to be keeping you from your goals—ask yourself these questions:

- *If I imagine doing the opposite of what I'm doing now, what fears or worries come up for me?*
- *What am I subconsciously protecting or preventing by maintaining these behaviors?*

The answers to these questions will expose a commitment you may feel, but not have even been aware of. Once you've identified your hidden commitments, the next question becomes: *What beliefs or assumptions are holding those commitments in place?*

4. Expose Your Big Assumptions

Behind every feeling you experience there is a triggering thought or a belief. Because our brains are built to save energy, most of these thoughts happen at lightning speed and live below the level of conscious thought. Here are two questions you can ask yourself to bring some of those thoughts into the light:

- *What assumptions make these commitments feel necessary?*
- *If these assumptions were false, how might my behavior or feelings change?*

5. Identify the Positive Intentions (What You're Fighting For)

In many cases those thoughts will involve trying to avoid something unpleasant like shame, guilt, conflict, or even hard work. To harness the productive power of paradox, you'll need to translate that avoidance into something positive you're fighting for. This is simply a matter of identifying the positive intentions underlying your competing commitments.

"Avoiding shame" could become "trying to be honorable."

"Avoiding conflict" might be translated to "improving relationships."

You get the idea. Think of your commitment as an internal value or goal you're drawn toward. This perspective shift moves you from a mindset of scarcity and fear—focused on fighting against or avoiding negative outcomes—to a mindset of abundance and hope. Recognizing the positive intentions reframes the paradox, allowing you to approach it constructively and creatively. Here are two questions that might help with this process:

- What valuable outcome is your commitment promoting?
- What positive intention or important value is your commitment protecting or pursuing?

When you have identified the positive outcome of your hidden commitment, you have the paradox in play. On one side you have the outcome or value you were intentionally seeking to begin with. On the other side you have an outcome that appears to contradict it. These are the two pillars of the suspension bridge you need to build. Paradox-awareness invites you to now uncover the innovation that will honor both.

For a downloadable worksheet to help you explore the paradox discovery process, visit the resources website here:
https://thelpc.com/tension-resources

Real-Life Applications: Seeing Yourself in Paradox

Consider the following composite character examples to see how liberating naming your paradoxes can be.

Emma's Leadership Scenario

Emma is the founder of a fast-growing online dating and matchmaking service. For months she's been waking up before her alarm with a knot in her stomach. Meetings leave her drained. Her team seems to be slipping—missing deadlines, making small but significant errors, and requiring more handholding than she ever expected.

Emma knows she's giving full effort, but privately she wonders: *Why am I working so hard and still feeling behind?*

The physical and emotional symptoms are clear. Fatigue. Tense team dynamics. A creeping sense of failure. But the cause? That's murky.

At first Emma attributes the stress to external factors: underperforming team members, unclear competitive threats, and an increase in demand. She asks a colleague she's worked with and trusted for years what constructive feedback he could offer her, and she's surprised by his response:

"You're always 10 steps ahead, Emma, but sometimes it's like you don't trust us to take even one."

It stings—and sticks.

Later that week, she journals about her frustration. A pattern emerges. She's micromanaging. She checks in constantly, reviews every deliverable, builds plans with little input. It's exhausting—and counterproductive.

Emma pauses, and asks herself:

- *What am I trying to achieve?*
  "I want our programs to succeed. I care deeply about the mission."
- *What part of me needs to control this—and what part wants to let go?*
  "I value structure. But I also value creativity. My team can't offer ideas if I'm already halfway down the road."

She names the tension: **Structure Versus Creativity**.

She's not wrong to want order. But her desire for precision is crowding out possibilities.

She experiments. She runs a Small Affordable Fast Experiment, a "SAFE" (more to come on SAFEs in Chapter 12). In the next team meeting, instead of presenting a detailed plan, she presents the challenge only—and invites input. The conversation is clumsy. There's a long silence. Someone makes a joke. But then, slowly, ideas surface. One suggestion sparks another. And when Emma responds with genuine curiosity, something shifts.

The energy changes.

The paradox doesn't disappear. Emma still feels the pull of control. She still wants to plan. But now she has language for what's happening inside. And that gives her room to pause, recalibrate, and choose.

She begins to hold both values at once—structure and creativity—not as enemies, but as collaborators in the work.

A Mid-Story Debrief

- **Emotional/Physical signals:** Anxiety, frustration, fatigue
- **Early interpretation:** *My team isn't stepping up.*
- **Reframe:** *I may be contributing to the bottleneck.*
- **Hidden commitment:** *If I don't keep everything under control, we'll fail.*

- **Paradox named:** Structure Versus Creativity
- **SAFE tested:** Withholding the plan to invite ideas
- **Result:** Awkward at first, but opened space for contribution
- **Status now:** Imperfect, ongoing—but more aware and less alone in the work

Carlos's Personal Scenario

Carlos manages a customer service division with about a dozen team members. He's always considered himself a "people-first" leader—approachable, empathetic, someone his team can count on.

But lately, things feel off.

He dreads performance check-ins. Two team members have missed targets for three months straight. Another has quietly started job hunting. Carlos spends hours in one-on-one coaching conversations, but nothing changes. He feels stuck. Worse—he feels like a fraud.

One night after work, Carlos vents to a friend:

"I give them everything I've got. I listen, I support, I coach. But they're still not getting results. How am I supposed to hold people accountable without turning into a tyrant?"

The question lingers. He doesn't want to be the kind of boss who rules with fear. But his current approach just isn't working.

The paradox creeps in.

Carlos begins journaling—not daily, but often enough to notice patterns. He's avoiding direct feedback. He holds back in meetings. He sugarcoats performance issues because he doesn't want to hurt anyone's confidence or seem hypocritical.

Eventually, he names the tension: **Accountability Versus Empathy**.

He wants to believe both are possible. But they feel mutually exclusive. He thinks:

If I'm too soft, I lose credibility. But if I push too hard, I betray my values.

He reflects on a hidden belief:

If I really cared about people, I wouldn't pressure them.

And he tests that belief. What if empathy isn't the absence of expectations, but the presence of clarity and care?

Carlos tries a small experiment.

In a one-on-one with an underperforming rep, he says:

"I want you to succeed, and I also owe you clarity. You're falling short of expectations. Let's talk about what support you need—and what accountability looks like moving forward."

The rep doesn't get defensive. In fact, he seems relieved. No more guessing. Just honesty—with dignity.

It's not perfect. The habit of over-softening returns. But Carlos has new language—and a new lens. His empathy isn't a liability. It's an asset, as long as it walks hand-in-hand with clarity.

Debrief

- **Emotional signals:** Frustration, self-doubt, fatigue
- **Early interpretation:** *I'm failing my team.*
- **Reframe:** *Avoiding clarity may be causing more harm than I think.*
- **Hidden commitment:** *If I hold people accountable, I'm betraying my values.*
- **Paradox named:** Accountability Versus Empathy
- **SAFE tested:** Honest, caring performance conversation
- **Result:** Improved clarity, deeper trust
- **Status now:** Still growing—but with a new compass

Navigating Organizational Constraints and Hierarchical Tensions

Sometimes, the tension or confusion you're experiencing arises because your goals are not aligned with others in your organization, particularly senior leaders who sit above you in an org chart. Let me offer an illustration.

A friend of mine is a collegiate soccer coach who is a remarkable and effective leader. His program has consistently produced national championship teams, academic excellence far surpassing other teams at the university, and alumni who are exemplary in their personal and professional lives. He is eager to expand the level of competition available to his players and the contribution of the program to the broader goals and mission of the university.

Despite his successes, my friend regularly feels trapped, blocked, and frustrated because the university administrators directly above him simply don't share his goals for the team. Whether the team wins or loses is irrelevant to the things those administrators care about and measure—things like graduation rates and administrative work reduction. The goal disconnect is compounded by a departmental culture where gaslighting, retribution, and passive aggression are standard mechanisms of control, but misaligned goals are the root problem.

Paradox-awareness is a powerful catalyst for reaching your goals only when your team is aligned about what the real goals are.

For my friend to keep his job and his sanity, he has to focus his efforts within the scope of his control. Without organizational alignment, he won't be able to achieve his highest aspirations for the team no matter how compelling they may be.

He may incrementally improve his own direct relationships with administrators.

He can work to persuade them to share his goals for the team.

He could even try to influence the culture of the department for the better.

But in the end, he has to focus his efforts within his own field of action.

What I've described is a common reality for many people in a mid-level leadership role. This is why goal clarity is the first step in The Leadership Progress Cycle. Paradox-awareness is a powerful catalyst for reaching your goals *only* when your team is aligned about what the real goals are.

Supplemental Tools to Surface Hidden Thoughts

In addition to the process described above, here are a few additional battle-tested techniques that may accelerate your efforts to surface the subconscious beliefs fueling the tension you feel. As with the adapted

Immunity to Change model, these tools are inspired by positive psychology and cognitive-behavioral insights:

- **Reflective Journaling**

  Write down the situation, your emotions, and your immediate thoughts. Challenge these thoughts by asking: *Is this entirely true? What are other perspectives?*

- **ABCDE Method**

  This is adapted from cognitive-behavioral therapy by Martin Seligman.

  > **A** – Activating event: Describe what's causing stress.
  > **B** – Belief: Capture your automatic assumptions.
  > **C** – Consequence: Notice resulting emotions and actions.
  > **D** – Disputation: Challenge your beliefs—are they valid?
  > **E** – Effective new thinking: Adopt a more empowering, realistic view.

- **Mindfulness and Meditation**

  Regular mindfulness practices such as focused breathing or guided meditation help you observe emotions without immediate reaction, creating space to explore underlying tensions and beliefs.

Facing Challenges: Persevering Through the Tension

Naming paradoxes is courageous work, so you should expect challenges:

- You might resist facing uncomfortable truths.
- Old habits of binary thinking might tempt you toward simpler, ineffective solutions.
- Emotional discomfort may initially intensify before clarity emerges.

Persevere. Each paradox named makes you stronger, wiser, and more resilient.

Who You Become

Regularly naming and engaging your paradoxes transforms you into a paradox-aware leader—flexible, adaptable, and insightful. You'll begin to confidently turn friction into forward momentum. Your decisions will embody nuanced wisdom, and your relationships will deepen through trust and balance. Where others see conflict, you will learn to see possibility. Like a bridge spanning two cliffs, your paradox-aware mindset allows you to build where others retreat.

Paradoxes you've once feared will become your greatest sources of growth and innovation.

Key Takeaways

- **Negative emotions like anxiety, frustration, and guilt are often signals of a paradox in play.** When those feelings persist without a clear source, it's time to look deeper.
- **Unproductive behaviors that keep you stuck are often driven by hidden commitments.** Identifying these behaviors helps uncover what you're unconsciously protecting or avoiding.
- **You play a part in your stuck patterns.** While it's tempting to blame external forces, real progress starts by recognizing your own role in what's not working.
- **Competing commitments often reflect core values in tension.** By exploring your assumptions and reframing them as positive intentions, you can name both sides of the paradox.
- **Clarity begins when you move from *What am I avoiding?* to *What am I fighting for?*** This shift opens the door to abundance-oriented, paradox-aware solutions.
- **You need clear goals first.** Paradox-awareness catalyzes progress only if you know where you want to go.
- **Paradox-aware leadership begins with internal clarity.** When you can name the truths pulling you in opposite directions, you become capable of crafting more innovative and resilient paths forward.

CHAPTER 12

Applying Paradox-Awareness with The Leadership Progress Cycle

In the previous chapter, you learned tools for uncovering the paradoxes shaping your leadership challenges. You've done the work: mapped your paradox, clarified the tension, named the values in conflict. This chapter gives you a simple process for working with paradoxes once you name them: The Leadership Progress Cycle (LPC).

The LPC is a four-step model for systematically transforming paradox-awareness into meaningful innovation. Each step draws on the wisdom of thought leaders who have studied how individuals and organizations thrive by engaging paradox rather than resolving it.

These are the four steps:

1. Set goals.
2. Identify barriers.
3. Experiment (via SAFEs: Small Affordable Fast Experiments).
4. Evaluate results.

Here's how each step works:

Step 1: Clarify Goals

Paradoxes only present themselves when you're trying to accomplish something important. It's always in the context of pursuing a goal that you experience the tug of competing values, goods, or necessary elements. If you've already identified a paradox, you might assume that you're already clear about your goals. My experience indicates that many individuals and teams don't actually have goal clarity.

Clarifying goals helps surface situations where people on the same team have conflicting goals. It calls attention to goals that are too vague to be actionable. It reveals when teams have not agreed on how they will measure progress and helps them accomplish that necessary step. Goal clarification is an essential prerequisite. Chapters 13 and 14 show how paradox-aware goal setting works.

Leaders who set paradox-aware goals avoid limiting false choices. Roger Martin, in his book *The Opposable Mind*, champions this approach. He shows how effective leaders don't collapse tension by picking one side—they embrace it, asking, "How might we achieve both?" He calls this mindset "integrative thinking." For example: Instead of asking, "Should we prioritize profit or purpose?" paradox-aware leaders ask, "How might we build profitability *through* purpose?"

Step 2: Identify Barriers

With goals set, the next step is to uncover what's in the way. External constraints are part of the picture, but internal barriers are much more consequential.

Chapter 11 showed how the adapted Immunity to Change model can surface subconscious commitments and limiting assumptions that sabotage progress. Leaders often hold hidden beliefs that keep them locked in old patterns.

To review, you ask yourself:

- *What behaviors or avoidance patterns are keeping me from progress?*

- *What fears or commitments are these behaviors protecting?*
- *What assumptions make those fears feel necessary?*

This step allows you to surface your own "immunity" to change. Progress always requires change. This step helps you uncover the hidden logic behind your own resistance, name it, and address it.

Step 3: Experiment

Breakthroughs rarely come from one-time epiphanies. They emerge from experimentation.

Wendy Smith and Marianne Lewis, in their book *Both/And Thinking*, offer a bit of crucial wisdom in this regard. They advocate for small, intentional steps into the unknown. Their research shows that "both/and" thinking is sustained through active learning and adjustment.

The best way to learn and fine-tune is with Small Affordable Fast Experiments (SAFEs). They let you test paradox-aware strategies quickly and with low risk.

Questions to ask:

- *What small pilot could I run to test a solution that honors both sides?*
- *What immediate action would stretch and test our current assumptions?*

Step 4: Measure Results

As experiments unfold, you need a way to measure whether you're getting closer to your goals. For the long-term, you need to also pay attention to whether your progress honors both values in tension.

Barry Johnson, in his book *Polarity Management*, offers a powerful evaluation tool that he calls polarity mapping. Here's the gist of this practice:

- Visualize the upsides and downsides of both poles.
- Monitor drift toward overemphasis on one side.
- Adjust dynamically and iteratively.

This disciplined reflection ensures paradox-aware solutions don't slip back into false tradeoffs.

Case Studies: Innovating Through Paradox

To make this process feel practical, here are three verifiable case studies of leaders who successfully moved their teams forward using the pattern of The Leadership Progress Cycle.

Case Study 1: San Antonio Police Department

Over many years of working with and providing training for public libraries, I've learned a lot about the difficulties of people experiencing homelessness, including addiction and serious mental illness. In that context, I love the work of the San Antonio Police Department (SAPD) that came to national attention through the HBO documentary *Ernie & Joe: Crisis Cops*.

In 2008, SAPD launched its Mental Health Unit with a bold experiment: Assign specially trained officers to respond to mental health crises with de-escalation, empathy, and connection, not force. Officers like Joe Smarro and Ernie Stevens were tasked with an unconventional goal: *Build trust, not control.* This broke sharply from the traditional policing mindset.

1. **Clarify Goals:** The unit's aim was clear but paradoxical: Reduce arrests and hospitalizations *while* improving community safety. This was a radical goal in a policing culture focused on compliance and control.
2. **Identify Barriers:** SAPD leadership recognized that the real barriers weren't just policy, but deep-rooted assumptions: that escalation equals effectiveness, that force equals safety, and that mental illness is a threat.
3. **Experiment (SAFEs):** Rather than overhaul the department overnight, SAPD trained a small team to pilot new approaches. These officers responded without flashing lights or uniforms and were trained to spend *time*—sometimes hours—with

individuals in crisis. They partnered with social workers and built relationships with local care providers.

4. **Measure Results:** The outcomes were transformative. Officers diverted thousands of individuals from jail to care. SAPD estimates that in the first 10 years, it saved over $50 million in reduced incarceration and hospitalization costs. But more importantly, it redefined what public safety could look like: compassionate, patient, and human.

This approach continues to inspire public sector leaders navigating these complex social tensions. It reminds us that meaningful change often starts with small, values-driven experiments—especially when they challenge entrenched systems.

Case Study 2: Netflix

I remember the first time a friend told me about this new service he was loving. It saved him a trip to Blockbuster by mailing him exactly the DVDs he wanted to watch. He was delighted to pay for the subscription. When I learned that Reed Hastings, the founder of Netflix, was shifting to streaming, I thought it might kill his wildly popular DVD business. It did.

1. **Clarify Goals:** In the mid-2000s, Netflix saw the writing on the wall: Physical media had a shelf life. Their long-term goal became enabling *instant access to video entertainment*—a move that would cannibalize their own DVD business.

2. **Identify Barriers:** Internally, the challenge was shifting from a logistics-centered company to a tech-centered one. The culture, customer base, and revenue model were all deeply tied to DVDs. Externally, broadband speeds were inconsistent, and most users still thought of "streaming" as an unreliable novelty.

3. **Experiment (SAFEs):** Rather than forcing the change, Netflix quietly launched its streaming option alongside its DVD model, giving users a low-risk way to try it. They tracked viewing habits, gathered user feedback, and steadily invested in infrastructure and licensing.

4. **Measure Results:** As data confirmed user enthusiasm, Netflix gradually de-emphasized physical media. By 2010, the company had rebranded itself around streaming, and in 2013, it launched original content like *House of Cards*. That SAFE experiment had grown into a global platform that reshaped the entire entertainment industry.

The leadership lesson? Even seismic reinventions can begin with experiments small enough to test without burning the ship. Even though Netflix leadership could see where they needed to go, they were steady and methodical about how they got there.

Case Study 3: Shopify

From the pandemic to the present, I've watched teams across industries wrestle with the challenges of remote work. A tension emerged between autonomy (well served by remote working) and unity (helped along with in-office work). The chair of the board at Niche Academy told us we were fools to continue to allow remote work and there was logic to his argument. Having grappled myself with how to preserve autonomy *and* build team cohesion, I was impressed with the approach taken by Shopify.

1. **Clarify Goals:** Faced with pandemic uncertainty, Shopify committed to becoming a fully remote organization. Their goal wasn't just continuity—it was to build a *more flexible, resilient, and globally inclusive workforce.*
2. **Identify Barriers:** Like many companies, Shopify had a deep-rooted office culture and physical infrastructure. There were also fears about innovation lagging without face-to-face collaboration.
3. **Experiment (SAFEs):** Instead of issuing top-down directives, Shopify piloted new tools and communication rhythms. They built internal teams to study engagement patterns, tested asynchronous workflows, and invited feedback from employees across departments.

4. **Measure Results:** These early experiments yielded strong internal adoption and revealed productivity gains in many areas. More importantly, Shopify continued to evolve its approach, adapting to employee needs while staying true to its flexible-first philosophy.

Shopify's leadership didn't pretend to have all the answers. They treated culture design as a living process—just as paradox-aware leaders must do when navigating change.

Applying This Process to Your Own Paradoxes

Keeping in mind these noteworthy examples of how The Leadership Progress Cycle fuels innovation, take a minute now to test your own thought process. With practice, you will become the kind of leader who sees both the forest *and* the trees—and finds a path forward through both. Imagine yourself in the following scenarios and brainstorm how you might respond.

Scenario 1: Autonomy Versus Belonging

Imagine yourself leading a team that is initially facing mandated office returns as a binary choice: flexibility sacrificed for team cohesion, or cohesion sacrificed for individual flexibility. Using integrative thinking, you ask, "How might we ensure deep personal autonomy while simultaneously fostering genuine team belonging?"

What experiments might you try?

Possible ideas:

- Hybrid schedules customized by teams
- Periodic in-person collaboration events balanced by remote work flexibility
- Tools and practices specifically designed to build belonging online (virtual team lunches, recognition platforms, collaborative decision-making tools)

Example 2: Speed-to-Market Versus Product Reliability

Imagine yourself as a startup founder stuck choosing between rapid product releases and rigorous reliability testing. By framing the paradox as "How might we rapidly deliver market-leading innovations while maintaining exceptional product reliability?" what experiments might you try?

Possible ideas:

- A "minimum lovable product" approach instead of a "minimum viable product," emphasizing core reliability without slowing down innovation.
- Establishing rapid, iterative user-testing cycles integrated seamlessly with product development.

Innovation Is Paradox in Motion

When you name a paradox, you can feel confident that you are not neglecting something important to your situation. When you move through The Leadership Progress Cycle, you transform that complexity into creative action.

To recap, you don't need to pick sides. You need to:

- Clarify your goals.
- Identify internal and external barriers.
- Run SAFEs.
- Evaluate the results and revisit your goals.

Instead of being stuck in either/or dilemmas, you now see tensions as opportunities for meaningful innovation. You no longer need to choose between autonomy or belonging, speed or reliability, profitability or purpose. You have learned how to create innovative solutions that embrace both fully.

As a paradox-aware leader, you don't run from complexity—you embrace it. You're comfortable operating within tension, using it as a catalyst for powerful, novel, breakthrough solutions. By consciously leaning into these paradoxes, you transform tensions from sources of anxiety into engines of creativity.

The best leaders don't resolve paradoxes—they thrive in them. Now you can too.

Key Takeaways

- **The Leadership Progress Cycle** offers a structured approach to navigating paradox through four iterative steps: **(1) Clarify Goals, (2) Identify Barriers, (3) Experiment (SAFEs), and (4) Measure Results**.
- **Great leaders don't collapse tension**—they set goals that honor both sides of a paradox. This is also known as integrative thinking.
- **Hidden commitments and assumptions often block progress.** Drawing from *Immunity to Change* (Kegan and Lahey), leaders must surface these inner barriers to create real movement.
- **Small Fast Affordable Experiments (SAFEs)** enable low-risk testing of paradox-aware solutions. These are key to making progress in complexity.
- **Evaluating results requires attention to *balance*, not just success.** Tools like polarity mapping help track drift toward overemphasis on one pole.
- **You can use The Leadership Progress Cycle to address your own paradoxes** by framing tensions as "How might we…?" questions and crafting experiments that honor both values.
- **Innovation is rarely clean or binary.** It lives in motion and requires leaders willing to engage, learn, and iterate.

Part 4

Clarifying Your Goals

CHAPTER 13

Defining Your Personal Purpose

There is a right-angled bend in the Kennebec River between the shipyards at Bath, Maine, and the open Atlantic. On the sunlit summer day of our tour boat excursion, it looked wide and easy to navigate. The captain of our tour boat pointed out a lighthouse on the north shore of the bend that didn't have a light, only a bell. The captain explained that there are days when the fog is so thick, not even the light of a lighthouse can penetrate to guide ships safely through the channel. The bell provides a marker for captains to keep their bearings.

So too do good leaders need sure bearings to set a course for their teams. Before you can guide a team, you need to have your own clear sense of purpose and direction. Paradox-aware leadership requires a stamina, a hope, and a tolerance for discomfort that are only possible with a deep and sustaining sense of personal purpose.

The Problem of Drifting Leadership

Most leaders begin their journey in a fog of busyness. Meetings fill the calendar, emails stack up, and urgent tasks swallow the day. On the surface, life looks productive—yet under it, there's a hollow feeling. You wonder if all this effort is adding up to something that truly matters.

It's easy to confuse activity with progress. You might be moving fast, but without a clear sense of "why," even forward motion feels like drift. The result is fatigue without fulfillment, and leadership that reacts instead of inspires.

Imagining a More Compelling Future

But there is another possibility. Imagine waking up each day with clarity—a sense that your actions today are important steps toward a future you deeply want. Imagine leading not from obligation but from aspiration.

Viktor Frankl observed, "Those who have a 'why' to live can bear almost any 'how.'" Purpose is more than motivation—it is stamina, resilience, and direction. When you glimpse your "best possible self," you realize leadership doesn't begin with strategies or team goals. It begins with a vision of who you want to become.

A clear personal purpose makes the struggle and the sacrifice worthwhile. The activity that follows will help you define your purpose.

Activity: Write Your Purpose Statement

Use the following prompts to reflect and gather ideas for a first draft of your personal purpose statement:

- What would have to be true in your relationships for you to feel deeply connected and authentic?
- What choices would allow you to feel proud, healthy, and aligned with your values?
- What would make your work feel meaningful, energizing, and valuable to others? What would have to be true of your life generally to feel that you are mastering skills, in love with life, and energized each day?
- At the end of your life, what do you want to be able to say about yourself?

Once you've reflected on the questions above, distill your purpose into a single statement. If it's helpful, try using this format:

"To [core contribution] so that [desired impact or transformation]."

Here are two possible examples:

- "To build learning experiences that unlock confidence so that people can step into leadership roles with courage and clarity."
- "To create spaces of trust so that teams feel safe to innovate and take meaningful risks."

Helps and Hindrances

All of us have a sense of purpose and possibility influenced by voices that surround us—family, friends, influencers, educators, etc. Paradox-aware leaders are intentional about the guides they select for themselves. You have the power to select for yourself the mentors, friends, faith, books, podcasts, and practices you invite into your sphere. The more selective you are about your guides, the more aware you'll become of the influences already in play and the more power you'll have to dial those influences up or down.

My own sense of purpose is the most authentic example I have to offer:

I've chosen my faith as my most important influence. It frames my most important relationships as my primary source of happiness for the rest of my life and for an eternal life I expect to follow this one. I've chosen Jesus Christ as my primary role model.

In my study of leadership, I've found value in books and podcasts by people like Steven Covey, Brené Brown, Ben Hardy, Brendon Burchard, and C. S. Lewis.

For the last 15 years, I've had advice from a running buddy who reads widely, listens well, and thinks deeply. I have a wife who has been my ballast, sanctuary, and advocate for over 30 years.

These are a few of my allies. They encourage me, challenge me, and walk (or run) along beside me. Again, these are all influences I've chosen, not just by-products of where and when I was raised.

When you are intentional about selecting your guides and allies, you'll encounter adversaries too. An adversary is any thing or person that distracts you from your purpose. Distractions often present themselves as things that feel urgent but are not important. There is noise that will try to drown out your vision.

To find that noise, look no farther than the pocket where you keep your phone. *Harvard Business Review's* Arthur C. Brooks argues persuasively that our addiction to constant stimulation through our phones blocks us from deep reflection and the emergence of our sense of purpose. If you want to be happy, he says, you need to let yourself be bored from time to time. This triggers the part of our brain that does purpose-oriented thinking.

Appealing side tracks will fragment your focus. The writer Robert Brault said, "We are kept from our goal not by obstacles, but by a clear path to a lesser goal." For example: A leader might chase quarterly sales numbers at the expense of developing their team. The numbers look good in the short-term, but turnover spikes, morale drops, and the deeper purpose of building a sustainable, thriving culture is lost. Short-term wins can sometimes be a distraction.

Fear of failure will whisper that it's safer to stay comfortable than to risk meaningful growth. But meaningful growth requires risk.

All of these adversaries are real, but they are not insurmountable.

Common Obstacles to Living Your Purpose

If adversaries are the people and circumstances that distract from your purpose, obstacles are the rough terrain our journey passes through—the contrary aspects of the world and the bodies we live in.

One such obstacle is **forgetfulness**. Life gets loud, and without intentional practice, your purpose slips to the background.

Another is **fatigue**. Purposeful leadership requires energy. When you fall into survival mode, the long-term vision feels distant. Here is where rituals, allies, and self-reflection provide stamina.

A third is **vagueness**. A purpose that is only abstract feels noble but changes nothing. Purpose must be translated into clear goals and actions. Recall from Chapter 6 how qualitative and quantitative goals work together. The activity that follows is a tool for setting a personal compass point supported by a set of measurable milestones.

Activity: Best Possible Self Journal Entry

1. Imagine yourself **90 days from now,** having made tangible progress toward your vision. Describe what you feel, what you've achieved, and what mattered most.

    Then, working backwards from that vision, write down **three measurable goals** for the next 90 days.

    The measure could be as simple as a Yes/No—you did it or you didn't. It could also be a metric, something that measures how much progress you made.

2. Imagine yourself **12 months from now,** building on that momentum. What does your life look like now? What does it feel like to have achieved what you did?

    Working backwards from that vision, write down **three measurable goals** for the next 12 months.

Here's a sample of what a best possible self entry might look like:

Ninety days from now, I wake up feeling energized instead of drained. I've been consistent in setting aside time for reflection and exercise, and I notice my patience with my team has grown. I've led two projects that not only met deadlines but left people feeling proud of their contributions. The most meaningful part is that I see myself leading with calm clarity instead of constant reaction.

My three goals:

1. Twenty minutes of reflection at least five days a week
2. Intentional one-on-one conversations with each team member monthly
3. Reading a book on leadership development and applying one insight each week

This exercise turns your vision into specific, time-bound commitments. It shifts you from drifting and reacting into leading with intention.

Practices That Keep Purpose Alive

As you get into the routine of your journey, you will need daily habits to keep your vision fresh. Here are some daily rituals that can help keep your "why" alive:

- **Purpose Journaling**: This is a short daily reflection. At the end of the day write down three wins for that day—three specific indicators that you lived your purpose that day. Then write down three things you plan to do tomorrow that will also help you align or realign with your vision. I like to do this with pen and paper, but you can write them wherever works best for you.
- **Vision Boards**: Create a collage of images, words, or quotes. Post it somewhere you can see it every day. Images and words that keep your future in sight, reminding you not just of what you want but of why it matters. I keep mine on the wall of my clothes closet.
- **Mind Movies**: These are mental rehearsals that combine vivid imagery with positive emotion to rewire your brain toward your chosen future. A mind movie includes specific scenes with visual detail, sounds, smells, and even tactile sensations. They help you experience a future reality and, most importantly, what it feels like to live that reality. Mind movie review is part of my daily meditation routine.

Let me give you an example scene from one of my own mind movies:

I'm standing in a European train station. The arched glass ceiling curves high overhead. Metal trusses rise like the rib vault of a cathedral, and a giant station clock glows above the departure boards. I hear the conductor's whistle, the soft chatter of conversations in multiple languages, the steady rattle of my rolling luggage. A warm pastry smell wafts from a bakery to my left. Something about that moment whispers *freedom*—an invitation to explore, to meet new people, to pursue new ideas.

Returning intentionally and regularly to that single vivid scene fuels an extraordinary amount of my current motivation. It invites me to build a life with time freedom, financial margin, meaningful work, and global connection. Every time I picture it, it makes decisions clearer. Is this step moving me closer to or further from that future?

You have scenes like that too. Maybe they involve family, or a vibrant team you're mentoring, or a mission you're finally pursuing. The point is not the scene—it's the *feeling* and the values behind it.

- **Prayer/Meditation/Reflection Time**: This is space you intentionally create to be still, clear your mind, and allow your purpose to come to the fore. For me, and many others who teach and practice meditation, it's much less helpful to try to force yourself into reflection than it is to simply create space and allow it to emerge. You may want to use music to create the emotional context, or you may prefer stillness. Meditation techniques like breathing or muscle contraction and release may also be useful to you. You may want to dedicate space to create consistency. A regular time of day is also helpful. You may want to include a mind movie in your reflection time.

These aren't magic tricks or gimmicks. They're deliberate habits that bring you back—again and again—to center, meaning, and purpose. If these habits don't resonate with you, find others that do. You won't get traction without daily rituals that support and reinforce your vision.

What It Feels Like to Lead with Clarity

As you practice purpose, something shifts. Your actions stop orbiting around convenience and begin aligning with meaning. You no longer simply respond to what's urgent—you choose what's important. You stop leading from fear of failure and start leading from desire to contribute.

In a previous chapter, I shared the 2008 story of Howard Schultz, the Starbucks CEO who realized the company couldn't just be about selling coffee quickly (reactive to market demand). His deeper purpose was creating a "third place" between home and work where people felt community and belonging. By re-centering on that purpose, Starbucks became more than a coffee shop. It became a cultural institution.

When your vision is clear, your present begins to organize around it. You begin to act not from who you've been, but from who you're becoming. This is how you add resilience, clarity, and magnetism to your leadership. This is what inspires others to follow.

From Personal Purpose to Team Goals

You now have the tools to define your purpose and set effective personal goals. In the next chapter, we'll expand outward—from your personal purpose to your team's goals—exploring how to align collective vision with individual clarity.

Because once you know who you are and what you're striving for, you can lead others not from a place of pressure but from a place of possibility.

Key Takeaways

- **Purpose is the leader's compass.** Just as ships need bearings in fog, leaders need a clear "why" to navigate the noise of busyness and pressure. Without it, leadership drifts into reaction instead of inspiration.
- **Your purpose statement is your anchor.** Distilling your contribution and its impact into a single line gives clarity that fuels resilience, stamina, and direction.
- **Influences matter.** The voices you choose—mentors, faith, allies—shape your vision. Adversaries like distraction, lesser goals, and fear can easily pull you off course if you don't name them.

- **Obstacles are natural terrain.** Forgetfulness, fatigue, and vagueness are part of every leader's journey. Intentional practices and rituals keep purpose from slipping into the background.
- **Vision must translate into action.** Exercises like the *Best Possible Self Journal* transform abstract aspirations into tangible commitments that shift you from drifting to leading with intention.
- **Habits sustain clarity.** Journaling, vision boards, mind movies, and reflection time aren't gimmicks; they are disciplines that bring you back—again and again—to your "why."
- **Purpose inspires magnetism.** When you lead from clarity and contribution instead of convenience or fear, you create the kind of leadership that others want to follow.

CHAPTER 14

Setting Goals with Alignment

My business partner, Jeromy, and I had been running Niche Academy for about seven years. We had built a profitable little business, but we weren't seeing the growth we believed was possible. So we joined a group called Elite Entrepreneurs, a coaching and mentorship practice focused on helping businesses like ours get to the next level.

One of the first things Elite taught us was that every member of our team needed three explicitly defined and measurable goals every month and every quarter. We thought we might come up with those in an afternoon. It took weeks, in the end. But once we put it into practice, we began to see where our real bottlenecks were.

It didn't immediately catapult us to next-level growth, but the discipline of setting clear goals gave us traction. It forced us to move beyond activity for activity's sake and start testing whether our actions were actually moving us closer to the outcomes we cared about.

The first step in The Leadership Progress Cycle is setting goals, because goals are prerequisites to progress. It doesn't make any sense to talk about "progress" unless you have a destination. Your goals give you a destination and tell you how close you're getting. They organize the efforts of each member of your team and are the language used to align their efforts.

Paradox-Awareness in Action

Chapter 5 showed how alignment between personal and team goals is essential. People's individual ambitions—both professional and life goals—are not distractions, they are sources of fuel when integrated thoughtfully.

Chapter 6 explored the tension between measurable and qualitative goals and introduced frameworks like OKRs and SMART goals. Those tools provide a structured way to translate a qualitative vision— like *trust*, *innovation*, or *belonging*—into metrics that don't distort the very thing you're trying to achieve.

Chapter 8 revealed the creative power that's released when goal setting honors a productive tension between directional clarity from a leader and cocreation with contributions from every member of a team.

This chapter gives you specific activities for putting your awareness of each of those paradoxes into practice. It gives you a way to translate new understanding into experiments you can try immediately. It gives you activities for practicing each of the following:

1. Extending alignment across life, work, and team goals
2. Translating qualitative goals into meaningful measures
3. Recognizing and addressing situations when team members have contradictory goals

Aligning Life Goals, Work Goals, and Team Goals

In Chapter 5, we looked at how personal goals and team goals can be harmonized. When you're implementing that balance for your own team, it's helpful to think of three layers of alignment: (1) life goals, (2) work goals, and (3) team goals.

When alignment exists, people bring their whole selves to work. Their life goals fuel their work contributions, and their work goals clearly advance team success. When alignment breaks down, individuals live in constant trade-offs—fragmented, fatigued, and sometimes quietly disengaged.

Activity: The Overlap Map

This activity can be done either in **one-on-one settings** or as a **team exercise**, depending on what kind of openness and conversation you want to create.

1. Ask each person to write down three things:

    *   One *life goal* (something meaningful outside of work)
    *   One *work goal* (specific to their current role)
    *   One *team goal* (something that contributes to shared success)

2. Together, look at the overlaps and the tensions.

    Examples of overlaps:

    *   A life goal of running a marathon aligns with a work goal of building resilience and discipline, which fuels team stamina during a demanding project.
    *   A work goal of improving communication skills aligns with a life goal of becoming a better mentor to youth outside of work and directly supports a team goal of stronger collaboration.

    Examples of tensions:

    *   A life goal of going back to school competes with a team's need for full availability during product launch.
    *   A work goal of deep craftsmanship feels contradictory to a team goal of speed-to-market.

3. Use overlaps to reinforce complimentary goals and tensions, and as opportunities to uncover possible paradoxes and paradox-aware solutions. In the process you will also run into resource constraints. Time, money, and attention are all finite resources. The secret to innovation is recognizing that, even within constraints, multiple options are always available.

- If time is a limiting constraint, you might still offer flexible hours or shift responsibilities temporarily so someone can pursue education while still meeting core team needs.
- If money is tight, you still might reframe priorities by asking: What's the smallest investment that still moves this personal or work goal forward without compromising the team?
- If attention is divided, you can still look at sequencing priorities—acknowledging that not every goal can be pursued simultaneously, but most can be pursued eventually.

Alignment works best when it's not one-sided. When leaders share their own personal goals, they create space for team members to do the same. Reciprocal sharing builds trust. It signals to team members that they don't have to hide what matters most to them. This kind of transparency strengthens focus by creating more honest, efficient conversations about what people are really working toward.

In the process of going through this exercise, you will discover goals team members may not have shared before. The fact that you are interested in their life goals opens powerful possibilities.

At Niche Academy, we built this into our culture from the very beginning. In interviews and in one-on-one meetings, we made it a standard practice to keep open the possibility that Niche Academy might not be the best long-term fit for someone's aspirations. We wanted to know what their life plans were, and then do everything possible to put their work at Niche Academy on the critical path toward those goals.

That meant different things for different people. For one person, it meant tuition help with an online master's program. A mom with kids at home needed flexible hours. One member of the support team was interested in starting to work on some engineering tasks. Another wanted a pathway to a user interface design role that aligned with her degree program.

Our bet was simple: Even if someone eventually left Niche Academy, they would give us their very best work for as long as they were with us if we showed up as advocates and cheerleaders for their whole lives. And that bet paid off again and again. The trust and transparency that resulted created efficiencies that multiplied. People leaned in, gave their best, and stayed longer than they might have otherwise.

And when they did move on, they left as friends and allies, not just former employees. And more than one person who left came back before too long.

Alignment doesn't mean everyone's goals collapse into sameness. It means difference is acknowledged, surfaced, and coordinated—with trust and transparency as the foundation.

Finding Measures for Qualitative Goals

In Chapter 6, we explored how **qualitative and quantitative goals must remain in balance**. Quantitative goals provide structure and accountability, while qualitative goals provide meaning and direction. Without qualitative goals, numbers become hollow and can incentivize the wrong behaviors. Without quantitative goals, vision becomes vague and progress impossible to track.

Qualitative goals are usually durable—they describe enduring aspirations like trust, innovation, or belonging. They don't shift every quarter. Quantitative goals, by contrast, are more fluid. They evolve as circumstances change, providing fresh signals that indicate whether you are moving toward the qualitative goal.

The challenge is that qualitative outcomes can't be measured directly. You can't simply declare, "Trust went up 15 percent." What you can do is find **effective surrogate measures**—indicators that suggest progress toward the qualitative goal without distorting it. This is tricky work. Shallow metrics are easily gamed or misleading. Thoughtful measures clarify progress without losing sight of meaning.

To spark your imagination, the following are samplings of measurable indicators associated with a few common qualitative goals:

- **Team Trust:**
  - Participation in 360° feedback
  - Frequency of knowledge-sharing
  - Number of concerns raised and addressed
  - Retention within critical teams
- **Customer Trust:**
  - Repeat purchases
  - Renewal rates

- o Net Promoter Scores (standardized measure of customer loyalty)
- o Customer referrals
- **Innovation:**
  - o Number of experiments run
  - o Percentage of ideas tested to evaluation
  - o Lessons learned and documented
  - o Adoption of pilot projects
- **Belonging:**
  - o Voluntary cross-team collaboration
  - o Employee referrals
  - o Survey data on psychological safety
  - o Tenure relative to industry benchmarks

These are illustrations, not prescriptions. The point is that quantitative measures will and should vary across contexts, but they should always point back to the stable qualitative goal.

The following two activities will help you match good measures to your qualitative goals.

Activity 1: The Metric Alignment Audit

1. Choose one qualitative goal you've already identified.
2. Ask yourself: *What would it look like if this were alive in daily work?*
3. Translate those answers into observable behaviors or outcomes.
4. Select measures that reflect those signals.
5. Stress-test: Could this metric be gamed without fulfilling the real intent?

The goal is honesty, not perfection. Metrics are servants of meaning, not replacements for it.

Activity 2: The "Root Why"

For task-oriented teams (such as call centers, service desks, or operations groups), identifying the qualitative goal may be a challenge. Task-oriented team members often feel disconnected from higher-level qualitative goals. In these cases, you can start your conversation with the tasks themselves.

Identify a routine task (e.g., answering customer calls).

1. Ask: "Why does this matter?"
   Possible Answer: "Because customers get their questions answered."
2. Ask again: "Why does that matter?"
   Possible Answer: "Because it helps customers solve problems quickly."
3. Ask again: "Why does that matter?"
   Possible Answer: "Because it builds confidence and trust in our service."
4. Ask again: "Why does that matter?"
   Possible Answer: "Customers who trust us spend more and stay with us longer."

After three or more rounds, you may feel like an inquisitive four-year-old, but you often arrive at a root qualitative goal—something that is a self-evident benefit for the team or your customers.

The following scenario shows how paradox-aware goal setting produces better results for a task-oriented team. Notice how the process honors and aligns both qualitative and quantitative goals.

- The team is trained to answer incoming customer calls.
- One of their important metrics is Average Call Handle Time. Lower is considered better because agents help more customers, work more efficiently, and lower costs.
- When the team connects with customer trust as a root qualitative goal, they realize that agents sometimes rush through calls to keep handle time low. They feel pressured to end the interaction before the customer's problem is fully solved. They realize that, while the efficiency looks good on the dashboard, unresolved issues lead to repeat calls, frustrated customers, and declining trust.

- Collaboratively, the team identifies two alternative metrics: First Call Resolution and Customer Satisfaction after interaction. When they are accountable for these metrics, agents are incentivized to take the time necessary to solve the customer's issue thoroughly on the first call.

By tracing tasks down to their "root why," teams often discover that some current measures incentivize behaviors that work against the real qualitative goal. This insight allows them to refine tasks and choose more appropriate measures.

There are times, though, when teams don't have agreement on their qualitative goals.

When Qualitative Goals Are Contradictory

My wife has worked for almost 25 years on the staff of the BYU Men's Soccer team. The team leaders and the staff operate from a vision that includes furthering the mission of the university as a whole and its sponsoring institution, The Church of Jesus Christ of Latter Day Saints. In addition to excellence in their sport, players are expected to speak to youth groups and be highly visible representatives of the values of the school and the church. Those expectations draw the best out of the student athletes and turn their team participation into one of the most important aspects of their BYU experience.

An internal reorganization moved the men's soccer team into the Department of Student Life. The vision of administrators in this department is focused on improving the general student experience. Student Life administrators aren't interested in the success of the team or its impact beyond the campus. For them, the players are just 24 of the 30,000 students attending BYU, so things like international travel, fundraising, and exhibition games with high-profile opponents are logical cuts to reduce overhead.

The soccer staff and the Student Life administrators had different qualitative goals. Because those conflicting visions were not acknowledged or resolved, the gap produced years of conflict, frustration, and work at cross-purposes. For me, this story vividly illustrates what happens when members of the same team have different qualitative goals.

Specific circumstances are unique to each organization, but here are three common ways conflicting visions play out:

1. There is **no shared qualitative vision.** Possible indications include:
   - Teams choose metrics that optimize for competing ends (e.g., one group prioritizes efficiency while another prioritizes customer intimacy).
     - Leaders struggle to explain how day-to-day work connects to a larger purpose.
     - Departments celebrate achievements that don't add up to a coherent story of success.
2. There are **different interpretations of the same vision.** Here's what this might look like:
   - A product team defines "innovation" as launching new features quickly, while an operations team interprets innovation as streamlining internal processes.
   - Marketing describes "customer centricity" as brand storytelling, while support interprets it as faster response times.
   - Two groups use the same language but pursue goals that pull in opposite directions.
3. **The vision exists but is ignored.** This might look like:
   - A vision statement is widely known but has little influence on daily decisions ("the laminated poster problem").
   - Leaders talk about values like collaboration, but reward only individual performance.
   - Long-term aspirations are overshadowed by short-term firefighting.

As basic as qualitative goals are, it's not always obvious when team members have conflicting visions. Qualitative goals have an emotional component that creates personal investment so it's often uncomfortable to recognize conflicts or call attention to them. Here are some red flags to watch for if you think conflicting visions may be in play for your team:

- Interpersonal conflicts simmer unresolved for months or even years.
- Teams celebrate wins that cancel each other out.
- Metrics are gamed in ways that harm long-term outcomes.
- Turf wars erupt when progress is defined differently.
- You hear phrases like "That's not my problem."

Misaligned metrics can be negotiated. Differing work goals can be coordinated. But when people disagree on the *vision itself*—the "why" behind the work—it cuts to the heart of identity and purpose.

When leaders become aware of conflicting visions within their teams, many fall back on their own position of authority to get a quick resolution. But as Chapter 8 showed, if they skip the work of listening, cocreating, and surfacing real differences, they may win compliance and lose commitment. Directional clarity and cocreation are two sides of a leadership paradox. The best outcomes are reserved for leaders who find a way to honor both.

This activity gives you a way to address vision misalignment when you discover it within your team.

Activity: Vision Alignment Forum

Purpose: Create a safe space to surface contested interpretations of vision, clarify alignment, and decide on a shared path.

1. **Set the frame**: As a leader, you openly acknowledge that visions have diverged. You articulate an essential paradox for the moment: "We need both shared clarity and space to listen to the wisdom in this room."
2. **Invite stories**: Instead of abstract arguments, ask each person to describe a moment when they felt the vision most alive in their work. Stories reduce defensiveness and anchor conversation in lived experience.
3. **Surface differences**: Facilitate mapping of key themes. Where do the stories converge? Where do they diverge? Write these visibly.

4. **Name the tensions**: Are the differences true contradictions, or are they paradoxes (e.g., innovation as both speed and depth)? If paradox, frame both sides as essential.

5. **Cocreate options**: Invite proposals for how the vision could be phrased or embodied in ways that integrate diverse perspectives.

6. **Leader's role**: After discussion, you can propose or collaboratively draft the clarified vision—drawing on what has been heard. As a leader, you don't abdicate responsibility. You integrate the wisdom of the group into a direction that is both clear and co-owned.

This approach preserves psychological safety, gives people voice, and strengthens trust—even when not everyone gets their preferred wording or emphasis. Knowing that they have been heard gives people space to buy in or remove themselves as an obstacle.

Earned Clarity

Any of these activities—creating alignment between personal and team goals, honoring and aligning vision and metrics, or addressing contested visions—can feel like running a gauntlet. But when your team emerges with a clarified set of goals, you'll feel the difference.

- Metrics don't distort but illuminate.
- Alignment bridges life, work, and team goals.
- Vision is both cocreated and directionally clear.

That kind of clarity gives people energy, coherence, and conviction. Alignment of this kind is a manifestation of the superpower of paradox-aware leadership. And when vision alignment is not an option, it allows team members to part ways and pursue their own chosen path in good faith.

For my business partner, Jeromy, and me, the clarity of our process allowed for an open conversation when the day came that we really did have diverging visions for Niche Academy. When I left to start The Leadership Progress Cycle, we parted as close friends, each of us wanting success for the other.

Key Takeaways

- **Goals create traction.** Activity becomes progress only when it's directed toward a defined destination. Clear goals reveal whether effort is moving you closer to outcomes that matter.
- **Alignment strengthens commitment.** When life goals, work goals, and team goals reinforce one another, people bring their whole selves to work. Trust and transparency deepen when leaders invite reciprocal sharing.
- **Qualitative and quantitative goals need balance.** Qualitative goals provide enduring meaning; quantitative goals shift regularly to provide signals of progress. One without the other leads either to hollow numbers or vague aspirations.
- **Metrics should serve the mission.** Surrogate measures must reflect real behaviors and outcomes, not distort them. The best metrics illuminate; shallow metrics invite gaming and misalignment.
- **Root causes matter.** Tracing routine tasks back to their "root why" connects daily work to deeper qualitative goals. This prevents metrics from incentivizing behaviors that erode trust or loyalty.
- **Conflicting visions undermine progress.** Contradictions arise when there is no shared qualitative vision, when visions are interpreted differently, or when vision is ignored in practice. Each requires intentional recognition and resolution.
- **Vision alignment requires both cocreation and clarity.** Leaders who create space for open stories and dialogue, and then name a clear direction, foster psychological safety and genuine buy-in.
- **Earned clarity energizes teams.** When goals are measurable without distortion, aligned across layers, and rooted in a cocreated vision, people experience coherence, conviction, and renewed energy to move forward together.

Part 5

Conclusion

CHAPTER 15

Paradox Is Personal

You might have noticed by now that paradoxes have a sneaky habit of showing up when you least expect—or want—them. We usually experience paradoxes as disruptions—moments when the ground under our feet shifts unexpectedly. At work, it might be the tug between risk and security, between speaking your truth and maintaining harmony. At home, it could surface as the tension between your aspirations and obligations, between personal growth and the comfort of stability. Wherever they appear, paradoxes always bring discomfort, but they also carry a secret invitation: the chance to grow, adapt, and evolve.

The promise of paradox-aware leadership is not limited to your professional role. Leadership, after all, isn't compartmentalized neatly into office hours; it's fundamentally about leading yourself. Paradoxes, in their messy complexity, aren't just problems to be solved—they're opportunities for heroic growth, waiting quietly within the contradictions you face every day.

In this chapter, shift your lens inward and examine the paradoxes you've already encountered, perhaps unknowingly, in your personal journey. You will see how recognizing and bravely confronting these paradoxes can unlock new possibilities for your own life and leadership. This is a deeply personal endeavor, but the rewards are profound: greater resilience, deeper self-understanding, and an increased capacity for wise and compassionate action.

The Courage to See Clearly

If paradoxes promise such transformative possibilities, why do we spend so much energy avoiding them? The answer is straightforward and human: Our brains are designed to save energy, and paradox-awareness requires an energy investment. Human minds crave consistency. We're drawn to clean narratives and tidy endings. Contradictions upset this neat mental housekeeping; they introduce cognitive dissonance—a state our brains dislike so intensely that we'll go to great lengths to erase or resolve it.

Yet paradox-awareness begins precisely where you acknowledge and tolerate that discomfort. Paradox-awareness means admitting that life is rarely black-and-white and that genuine truths often exist as pairs that resist neat reconciliation. It's the recognition that your impulse toward certainty, although deeply understandable, may also limit your vision, your creativity, and your courage.

Let's try a reflection exercise. Consider a recent situation in your personal or professional life that caused significant discomfort or internal tension. Perhaps you felt caught between loyalty and honesty in a friendship, or torn between your desire for career advancement and your longing for more time with family. Pause to identify clearly: What were the competing values or principles pulling you in opposite directions? If you haven't already used the process outlined in Chapter 11, use that process to name a paradox you're experiencing.

- Perhaps it's **security versus adventure**, where you longed for stability but also craved change and excitement.
- Maybe you felt tension between **ambition and intimacy**, wanting to achieve but simultaneously yearning for simplicity and connection.
- Or you struggled with **accountability versus empathy**, finding it difficult to hold someone accountable without feeling harsh or uncompassionate.

Don't approach this as an exercise in self-criticism; it's an opportunity for new clarity and insight. Acknowledging the truth of both sides doesn't mean you have a solution immediately—it simply means you're now seeing clearly, perhaps for the first time, what's truly at stake.

The transformative promise of paradox-awareness begins right here, with this gentle moment of clarity. And though clarity may be uncomfortable, it is always preferable to the fog of avoidance. As the influential psychologist Carl Rogers put it, "The curious paradox is that when I accept myself just as I am, then I can change." Real growth doesn't begin in the soothing comfort of certainty—it starts when you courageously hold your contradictions, gently but firmly, and refuse the urge to escape them.

The sections ahead show how you can practically harness this discomfort and use paradox as a springboard to richer, more resilient living. For now, congratulate yourself on taking this courageous first step: You've dared to see your paradoxes clearly. This is the beginning of transformation.

Stuck Is Where Growth Hides

If you neglect something important to your goals, you will feel stuck. When you feel stuck, you're likely neglecting something important. The feeling of being stuck, either professionally or personally, almost always indicates you're caught within a hidden paradox. Your brain is wired to want a quick resolution. It will try to pick a side, or avoid the tension altogether—but therein lies the trap. Paradoxes aren't roadblocks; they're signals pointing directly to where your next breakthrough is hiding.

If you neglect something important to your goals, you will feel stuck. When you feel stuck, you're likely neglecting something important.

Think for a moment about a time you faced a significant decision that seemed impossible to resolve neatly. Perhaps it was a career crossroads: Should you stay in a secure but unfulfilling job, or pursue a risky but potentially rewarding opportunity? Maybe it was a personal relationship, where you felt torn between authenticity and harmony, between honesty and keeping the peace. Such dilemmas often appear as either/or choices—binary problems demanding decisive, once-and-for-all solutions.

Yet here's the essential insight: When you look closer, these moments of tension aren't either/or propositions at all. They're invitations to grow into something larger, something more expansive. Psychologists who draw from the insight of Carl Jung call this "holding the tension of opposites"—a paradoxical practice of living in uncertainty long enough for a deeper synthesis to emerge.

The theologian and developmental psychologist James Fowler described this as reaching a stage of "conjunctive faith," the capacity to embrace ambiguity and complexity without retreating to easy certainties.

Taoist traditions illustrate this through the concept of universal, interconnected, and complementary forces called yin and yang. This reminds us that seemingly opposing forces—light and dark, action and rest—depend on each other and can only exist in dynamic harmony.

What hidden paradoxes are waiting for your attention right now? What creative possibilities might unfold if you bravely choose to hold the tension instead of fleeing from it?

Leaning into Tension

Leaning into tension might sound about as appealing as leaning into an electric fence, yet that's exactly where real breakthroughs happen. There's a reason we use metaphors like "growing pains"—because discomfort is often the precursor to growth.

Marsha Linehan, creator of Dialectical Behavior Therapy, taught that true change requires us to embrace paradox: accepting reality fully, just as it is, even as you strive to alter it. On the surface, this might sound contradictory: How can you simultaneously accept something and seek to change it? Yet this paradox is at the heart of almost all meaningful transformations. Only when you acknowledge the full reality of your present—painful contradictions and all—can you move forward authentically toward meaningful change.

Consider for yourself: What tensions have you instinctively avoided because they felt too uncomfortable, too daunting? Could you try your own set of SAFEs—small experiments—to explore new ways to honor all parts of your paradox? Perhaps it's as simple as dedicating one meeting a week to explore alternative solutions or reserving personal reflection time to journal through your competing feelings. Remember, you don't have to solve everything immediately. Small, iterative steps can yield tremendous insight over time.

The Transformative Power of Paradox

As uncomfortable as paradoxes might feel, they carry an extraordinary transformative power—perhaps precisely because of the discomfort they provoke. In the Zen Buddhist tradition, monks meditate on paradoxical riddles known as "koans"—like "What is the sound of one hand clapping?"—precisely to jolt the mind out of habitual thought patterns. The confusion they feel isn't a distraction; it's the whole point. It creates space for insight and breakthroughs that conventional thinking would never allow.

Think of your own life as a series of personal koans, each paradox inviting you to step outside the comfortable illusion of black-and-white certainty. What personal paradox could be waiting for your own transformative embrace? Is there some aspect of yourself—perhaps vulnerability, a hidden desire, or a value you're secretly ashamed of—that might actually be the key to your greatest strength?

Paradox transforms us by inviting us into integration rather than fragmentation. When we can genuinely say, "yes, and . . ." to our contradictions, we become more whole, more capable, and more fully human.

Living Authentically in a Complex World

To live authentically is to embrace complexity, ambiguity, and paradox—not to shy away from them. Authenticity emerges not from presenting a carefully curated, simplified version of ourselves, but from honoring the multifaceted truth of who we are, tensions and contradictions included.

Psychologist Erik Erikson described life as a series of paradoxical tensions—trust versus mistrust, identity versus role confusion, integrity versus despair. Healthy development isn't about eliminating one side; it's about navigating and integrating both poles of each paradox. Similarly, James Fowler's model of spiritual growth describes reaching a stage where one can comfortably hold multiple truths simultaneously, recognizing the beauty and complexity inherent in contradictions.

Authenticity thrives precisely in the tension between conflicting truths. It's easy to see paradox as a problem; paradox-aware leaders see it as their most valuable tool for building genuine strength. They reject simplistic narratives of "either/or" in favor of a nuanced, resilient "both/and."

Authenticity in a complex world demands courage—the courage to question easy certainties, the courage to hold ambiguity patiently, and the courage to integrate our contradictions into a richer, fuller self. As philosopher Søren Kierkegaard wrote, life's tensions are "not something to be resolved, but something to be lived."

Imagine the profound relief of no longer needing to hide or simplify yourself. Imagine instead living from a place of radical honesty about your complexities, contradictions, and tensions. Paradox-aware leaders don't just tolerate these contradictions, they celebrate them. They recognize authenticity as the synthesis of apparent opposites—strong yet vulnerable, confident yet humble, driven yet deeply empathetic.

In your own life, consider this: How might your deepest contradictions be exactly what others most need to see and learn from? What if your willingness to embrace paradox authentically not only transforms you personally but also makes you precisely the leader your team, your family, and your community need?

Integrating Opposites

Carl Jung argued that true growth comes not from suppressing our contradictions but from integrating them. Jung's concept of the "shadow self" describes parts of ourselves we reject or hide, traits we deem unacceptable or weak. Jung believed that these neglected aspects often hold keys to our greatest strengths. "I'd rather be whole than good" is a popular paraphrase of a powerful Jungian concept—the acknowledgment that our authenticity depends on embracing the paradoxical truths within us.

What contradictory aspects of yourself do you reject or hide? How might these become sources of strength?

Navigating Life's Big Transitions

Life's biggest transitions often feel uncomfortable because they force us into a liminal state—a place Erik Erikson described as essential for growth. Erikson outlined life stages defined by opposing tensions—trust versus mistrust, identity versus role confusion, and integrity versus despair, among others. He saw these stages not as binary choices to resolve quickly, but as paradoxes that must be integrated to achieve maturity. Similarly, James Fowler's stages of faith describe spiritual maturity as a capacity to embrace ambiguity and paradox, recognizing that life's most profound truths can't be captured by simplistic either/or thinking.

Where are you currently experiencing liminality—feeling "betwixt and between"? How might this uncertainty become transformative?

Paradox-Awareness as a Daily Practice

Learning to navigate paradox isn't reserved for rare moments of existential crisis; it is a skill we can practice and develop daily. Instead of dismissing one side of a dilemma, this approach honors the legitimacy of competing perspectives and looks creatively for integration.

This practice isn't limited to major life decisions. Imagine everyday scenarios: A team leader hesitates to provide critical feedback, afraid to hurt feelings. Using paradox-awareness, they might acknowledge, "Yes, this feedback might be uncomfortable, and it's essential for growth." Or an individual facing conflict with a friend might say, "Yes, I'm upset by what happened, and I deeply value our relationship enough to work through it." Small acts of acknowledging dual truths become powerful steps toward healthier relationships, wiser decisions, and greater resilience.

Consider incorporating these simple reflection questions into your daily routine to deepen your paradox-awareness:

- *What competing values surfaced today?*
- *How can I honor multiple truths without defaulting to an easy answer?*

When paradox-awareness becomes a daily habit, you begin to see life's complexities not as frustrations or obstacles but as invitations to creative growth and deeper insight. The tensions themselves become your most reliable teachers, guiding you toward wisdom, balance, and a richer understanding of yourself and others.

Living Heroically in Paradox

Confronting paradox takes courage—the quiet, daily courage to stand calmly in uncertainty and to feel deeply the tensions of life, yet to resist the urge to simplify or escape. It requires vulnerability because you must admit that you don't have all the answers, and authenticity because you must acknowledge that your truths, however cherished, are not the only truths worth holding.

Consider the story of Nelson Mandela, whose life embodies paradox-aware heroism. Imprisoned for 27 years under a regime he opposed, Mandela emerged not hardened or vengeful, but strengthened by a powerful paradox: the ability to honor justice alongside forgiveness. He led South Africa through reconciliation, not because he abandoned justice in favor of harmony but because he recognized both as essential, inseparable truths. His leadership transformed a country precisely because he bravely confronted the paradox of holding oppressor and oppressed together in the same hopeful vision for a better future.

Another compelling example is Brené Brown, a researcher famous for exploring vulnerability and courage. Her work reveals the paradox that courage and vulnerability are not opposites, but they are inseparable. Brown's own life illustrates this truth: As a self-described "recovering perfectionist," she struggled to let herself be truly seen. But paradoxically, the more openly she shared her vulnerabilities, the more powerful her influence became, encouraging millions to live courageously authentic lives.

When you embrace paradox, you are following the path of heroes like Mandela and Brown—leaders who show us the transformative power of holding contradictions with grace. Your paradoxes might be less globally visible but they are no less meaningful. Perhaps your paradox is about honoring both your dreams and your family obligations, authenticity and professionalism, or maintaining stability while seeking meaningful change. Whatever your particular paradox, it holds the key to a deeper, stronger, and wiser version of yourself.

The Freedom of Paradox

Throughout this exploration, you've seen that paradox-awareness is not about resolving contradictions, nor is it about grudging compromise. It is about creative synthesis, courageous curiosity, and continual growth. It's a way of living fully—bravely—within the complexities that shape our personal and professional lives.

Every paradox you bravely confront enriches your understanding, adds depth to your character, and builds resilience. Each moment spent patiently navigating contradiction deepens your empathy, strengthens your relationships, and enhances your capacity for creative insight. You begin to find a profound freedom in not needing every tension to be neatly resolved, but instead accepting the discomfort, knowing it's the necessary friction for meaningful change and growth.

Paradox-aware leadership, at its core, is the recognition that life's most powerful insights lie not in easy answers but in courageous questioning, ongoing experimentation, and humble openness to multiple truths. Embrace paradox not as a problem to solve but as a hero's journey—your own journey of discovery, authenticity, and transformation.

Your paradoxes await—what new strengths and possibilities will you discover?

Key Takeaways

- **Paradoxes are invitations, not interruptions.** They often arrive unannounced, bringing discomfort, but they also signal opportunities for growth, resilience, and deeper wisdom.
- **Leadership isn't compartmentalized.** The paradoxes you face at work mirror those in your personal life. Learning to confront them in either sphere strengthens your capacity in both.
- **Clarity begins within.** Recognizing the tensions that pull at you—between risk and security, candor and harmony, ambition and stability—helps you lead yourself before leading others.

- **Growth comes through discomfort.** Feelings of anxiety, frustration, or guilt often reveal paradoxes at play. Facing them with courage transforms them from sources of stress into catalysts for self-understanding.
- **Paradox-aware leadership starts with self-leadership.** By bravely naming and confronting your own paradoxes, you expand your capacity for wise, compassionate, and innovative action.
- **Everyday leadership is paradoxical.** Whether it's navigating work-life balance, giving feedback, or making ethical decisions under pressure, daily leadership moments are shaped by paradox. Awareness enhances resilience and effectiveness.

Review Inquiry

Hey, it's Jared here.

I hope you've enjoyed the book, finding it both useful and fun. I have a favor to ask you.

Would you consider giving it a rating wherever you bought the book? Online book stores are more likely to promote a book when they feel good about its content, and reader reviews are a great barometer for a book's quality.

So please go to the website of wherever you bought the book, search for my name and the book title, and leave a review. If able, perhaps consider adding a picture of you holding the book. That increases the likelihood your review will be accepted!

Thanks in advance,

Jared Oates

Will You Share the Love?

Get this book for a friend, associate, or family member!

If you have found this book valuable and know others who would find it useful, consider buying them a copy as a gift. Special bulk discounts are available if you would like your whole team or organization to benefit from reading this. Just contact jared@thelpc.com or visit https://thelpc.com.

Would You Like Jared Oates to Speak to Your Organization?

Book Jared Now!

Jared Oates accepts a limited number of speaking/coaching/training engagements each year. To learn how you can bring his message to your organization, email jared@thelpc.com or visit https://thelpc.com.

About the Author

Jared Oates is the creator of The Leadership Progress Cycle, a simple, repeatable process for turning paradox-awareness into breakthrough solutions. He is the cofounder of Niche Academy, an online learning platform serving tens of thousands of highly engaged learners around the world.

Before his entrepreneurial turn, he taught himself to code and built software for companies like Symantec, Xactware, and SirsiDynix. He also earned a master's in English Rhetoric from Brigham Young University, a credential that has proven surprisingly useful in both writing and negotiating with teenagers.

As the son of a diplomat, he grew up living in places like Colombia, Germany, and Japan—which helps explain both his love of language and his irrational fascination with frequent flyer points. He and his wife have raised five children in Lindon, Utah, where faith, family, and community shape everything he does.

Jared can be reached at: https://thelpc.com